JOB HUNTING
MADE EASY

Dr. Carol Sonnenblick
Michaele Basciano
Kim Crabbe

LearningExpress
NEW YORK

Library of Congress Cataloging-in-Publication Data

Job hunting made easy.
    p.   cm.
    Includes index.
    ISBN 1-57685-119-2
    1. Job Hunting—United States. 2. Applications for positions.
HF5382.75.U6J6324   1997
650.14—dc21   97-11420
                                      CIP

Printed in the United States of America
9 8 7 6 5 4 3 2 1
First Edition

For Further Information
For information on LearningExpress, other LearningExpress products, or bulk sales,
please call or write to us at:
    LearningExpress®
    900 Broadway
    Suite 604
    New York, NY 10003
    212-995-2566

LearningExpress is an affiliated company of Random House, Inc.

Distributed to the retail trade by Random House, Inc., as agent for
LearningExpress, LLC
Visit LearningExpress on the World Wide Web at www.learnx.com

ISBN 1-57685-119-2

CONTENTS

INTRODUCTION

Welcome to the real world! At a time of tremendous change and upheaval, new technologies, and increasing opportunities, you find yourself entering a job market saturated with people out of work.

Some are professionals downsized by a changing corporate structure. Others are career changers in search of the perfect job. There are health care workers who have been restructured by a hospital depleted of funds. And then there are people like you: excited, hopeful, and scared to death to enter or re-enter the job market.

You have come to this book to seek answers. Where do I start? Whom do I call? Who would hire *me?* What do I put in my resume? What is this thing called *networking?* How do I write a cover letter?

Maybe you have just graduated from school. Or you might have been home with the kids and be about to re-enter the work force after a long absence. Or maybe you've been working in the same job for a long time and don't know how to go about looking for a new one. Whatever your circumstances might be, you will find the information in this book to be a concise, complete step-by-step guide designed to lead you through the process of successful job hunting.

HOW TO USE THIS BOOK

This book presents the *entire* process of job hunting in a logical, easy-to-use format.The chapters are designed so that you can discover the skills and knowledge needed to attain your goals in twenty easy steps.

You will begin the process with easy exercises that will lead you towards self-awareness and career decision-making. Once that is accomplished, you will develop the tools necessary to conduct your job search. You will develop a resume and effective cover letters. You will discover the best ways to job hunt. You will learn about interviewing techniques and appropriate follow-up activities. You will learn how to use the Internet to conduct a high-tech job search.

Each chapter covers just one step in the process. If your time is limited—and whose isn't—you can read a chapter a day in half an hour or so, and cover all the job-hunting basics in less than a month. Be sure to take the time, though, to do the activities in each chapter. They're not busywork—they're indispensable steps you need to take to get the job you want.

WHAT THIS BOOK CAN DO FOR YOU

There are many steps involved in the process. You will have to devote time, energy, and determination in seeing it through. So what's in that gold-wrapped box at the end of the rainbow?

A Job

Not just any job, mind you. But one that fits you like a glove, that is custom-tailored to your exact measurements. By the end of this book, you will have discovered many important things about yourself and the job market. You will know which jobs best suit your skills, needs, and values. You will discover who is hiring and what they are looking for. You will know the most effective ways to spend your time job hunting. You will be able to match your strengths with the requirements of the job you seek. In the end, you will get to say, "*Yes*, I accept the position."

A Career Path

The process of discovering yourself, what you like, what you're good at, and what you value, is the first step in planning your future. The job you get after reading this book will by no means be your last. Knowing how your particular personality and abilities fit into the workplace will lead to the path that is right for you. Which path you choose will affect all your future choices and opportunities. Know who you are, and you'll get to the place where you want to be.

Strength

You go to the gym to become strong and fit. Certainly, this is something you can do in your basement with a bench, a rack, and a few hundred pounds of free weights. But in the gym, you become competitive. There's no way you're going to let Adonis over there lift more weight and do more reps than you. And so it is in the job market. There are fifty job seekers out there vying for the same space you want to occupy. How will you out-muscle them? By flexing your job-hunting savvy, by loading your resume with heavy-duty action verbs, and by being the sharpest, most focused candidate an employer will ever come across. If knowledge is power, then you will be the Hercules of Job Seekers.

Life Lessons

What you learn here, you will use throughout the rest of your professional life. Most people go through their lives as victims of circumstance. They change jobs according to the number of pink slips they receive, or choose a career based on what Jack, their next door neighbor, told them about opportunities in typewriter repair. The process of evaluating your strengths, the job market, your interviewing skills, and how you will find your next job is one you will use throughout the rest of your life.

As your career grows in scope and responsibility, the process becomes more sophisticated; nevertheless, the steps are the same. Most people will change jobs seven to ten times during their working years, and many will make complete career changes at least four of those times.

So, where will you be ten years from now? How many jobs and how many career changes will you have made by that time? The answer is unimportant. What is important is that you will know how to apply the process in an organized, focused manner. Your career will not be haphazard. It will be organized and balanced with knowledge and strength.

You will take charge and plan your course of action. And by learning the process now, you will reap all the benefits of the very best job for you.

"Just imagine,
Just imagine:
Imagine all the things that you could be,
And all the places you could go."
—*Barney the Dinosaur*

CHAPTER | 1

Before you look for a job, you need to know what you're looking for. So roll up your sleeves and get ready to explore—you! The exercises in this chapter are the first step in your job hunting process. They'll help you discover your interests, skills, and values. When you complete this chapter and all its exercises, you will know what you need and want in a job.

GETTING TO KNOW YOU
YOUR INTERESTS, SKILLS, AND VALUES

Career decision-making, the kind that leads to a successful, satisfying work life, cannot be accomplished in a few moments of introspection or conversation. It is, in effect, a *process*.

It precedes all other steps in the job-hunting process and is an integral piece to the puzzle of finding the right job. You cannot choose a career, write a resume, or do well in interviews without first knowing who you are and where you fit into the world of work. There is a direct correlation between how well you know yourself and how successful and happy you are.

TRUE STORY

Know Thyself, or You Won't Get Far

Darren was referred to a career counselor by his mother, who was wondering if she should continue to pay his college tuition. Darren was 19 and about to enter his sophomore year. He was polite, articulate, bright, and earnest, but he was ambivalent about remaining in school. He was not doing well in his classes, and he was anxious to get a job and buy a car. However, most of his friends, including his girlfriend, went to the same college he attended, and he wanted to be with them.

The career counselor at college gave Darren a comprehensive career assessment. When she read the results, she was at a complete loss. Darren's results showed that he had no special interests, no outstanding skills or abilities, and the only value he placed in work was the ability to maintain an average standard of living. He was adamant about not caring about work or school. It wasn't that he was unwilling to work hard, only that he didn't care where or how he did it.

Darren stayed in school that semester, eventually flunking out and taking a job he heard about through a friend. After three months of discontent, he talked his mother into funding one more semester of college, which again resulted in failing grades. Three years later, Darren has been in and out of jobs, searching for some success that remains elusive.

Look at Darren's story. Darren's inability or unwillingness to discover his skills, values, and interests resulted in discontent and a lack of focus. Don't let this happen to you. Time and time again, people go to career counselors seeking an answer to the question, "How can I find the perfect job and live happily ever after?" Only one person can really answer that question—you.

There is no *perfect* job. But there can be a perfect, or near-perfect, match—a job that matches your best skills and values with work that interests you, that enables you to use the best of what you've got for your personal satisfaction and reward.

THE SELF-ASSESSMENT PROCESS

There are three major steps involved in self-assessment:

1. Exploring your interests
2. Defining your skills and abilities
3. Clarifying your values

The following exercises are designed to help you explore this process. At the conclusion, you'll synthesize the information, pulling out your strongest interests, skills, and values. Take your time and answer each question as thoughtfully and candidly as possible.

INTERESTS

This section will help you to identify your interests—those things you *like* to do, which is not necessarily the same as those things you are *capable* of doing.

The Exercise

The *Guide for Occupational Exploration*, published by the U.S. Department of Labor (1979) took all jobs in the United States and organized them into twelve categories based on worker interest. Review each of those categories below and place a check next to each one that relates to your own interests. Then, go back and pick out three of your strongest interests, numbering them in order of importance.

_____ **Artistic:** creative expression of feelings or ideas
_____ **Scientific:** discovering, collecting, and analyzing information about the natural world, and applying scientific research findings to problems in medicine, the life sciences, and the natural sciences
_____ **Plants and Animals:** working with plants and animals, usually outdoors
_____ **Protective:** using authority to protect people and property
_____ **Mechanical:** applying mechanical principles to practical situations by use of machines or hand tools

_____ **Industrial:** repetitive, concrete, organized activities done in a factory setting

_____ **Business Detail:** organized, clearly defined activities requiring accuracy and attention to details, primarily in an office setting

_____ **Selling:** bringing others to a particular point of view by personal persuasion, using sales and promotion techniques

_____ **Accommodating:** catering to the wishes and needs of others, usually on a one-to-one basis

_____ **Humanitarian:** helping others with their mental, spiritual, social, physical, or vocational needs

_____ **Leading and Influencing:** leading and influencing others by using high-level verbal or numerical abilities

_____ **Physical Performing:** physical activities performed before an audience

The Results

To the best of your ability, list in order of importance your three strongest interests:

1. _____

2. _____

3. _____

Questions to Consider

1. Of the interests I chose, does my present job or course of study allow me to get involved in or express these interests? Explain.

2. Could I be happy if my job _did not_ involve these interests? (For example, if you chose an interest in plants and animals, could you be happy as an accountant?)

3. Of the careers with which I am familiar, which ones would make a good match with my interests?

4. In what ways can I combine the things I like to do in choosing a job or career? (For instance, if your greatest interests were in the artistic and humanitarian categories, you might choose a career as an art therapist.)

SKILLS AND ABILITIES

Next, you need to begin to think about your answer to one of the most often asked interview questions: "What are your greatest strengths?" Admittedly, it's not an easy question for anyone to answer. Don't panic; just continue on with the next exercise, which will bring you closer to the answer by helping you discover what you are good at.

The Exercise

The following skills and abilities are grouped according to eight major categories: **Verbal, Social, Numerical, Investigative, Manual/Physical, Creative, Working with Others,** and **Administrative.** Just put a check mark next to the three skills categories that you think best describe you.

____ **Verbal:** I am a very good communicator. I find it easy to talk to people. Friends have told me I could sell anybody anything. I feel I'm good at leading people to my point of view in a discussion. My writing skills are good. I express myself well in all forms of communication.

____ **Social:** I am comfortable in most social situations. I have a natural way with people, and I'm able to quickly put them at ease. I like to dress appropriately and professionally. I enjoy helping people with their problems and providing them with the assistance they require. I'm a "people" person, and I'm generally considered a friendly face in the crowd.

____ **Numerical:** I'm really good with numbers. I can calculate sums quickly and accurately. I've always been good at math, and my teachers have told me I'm a natural with numerical problems. I liketo research analytical data and solve problems. I'm also good with computers and enjoy using them.

_____ **Investigative:** I am skilled with gathering information and presenting solutions. I have a scientific nature and have always done well in school science fairs. I'm a fairly good technician, working with the practical or mechanical side of things.

_____ **Manual/Physical:** I've always had a talent for using my hands and creating things. I liked shop classes, learning how to use the woodworking machines and other mechanical tools. I am physically strong and enjoy working outdoors.

_____ **Working with Others:** I like to work with others in various ways, such as managing other people, instructing them, or leading them in ways to improve their performance. I would make a good teacher or supervisor. I like to help other people and provide information and counseling when needed.

_____ **Administrative:** My organizational skills have always been admired by teachers and managers. I can easily handle a large workload and can plan out the steps necessary to complete the job. I have no problems making decisions and sticking to them.

_____ **Creative:** I am very talented in the creative arts. I have artistic tendencies (in drawing, painting, designing, sculpting, singing, dancing, etc.) I have a wonderful imagination, and I can take ideas and make new creative forms.

The Results

Review the three skills categories you have checked. List them here in order of importance:

1. _____

2. _____

3. _____

Questions to Consider

1. What additional skills and abilities would I like to acquire?

2. Is there a conflict between my greatest strength and what I always wanted to do? For instance, have I always wanted to be a ballerina, but my greatest strength was mathematics?

3. If the career I choose requires additional skills than I presently possess, am I prepared and able to acquire them?

4. What have I learned about my skills and abilities that I did not know before and how might this insight help me in my career plans?

VALUES

Values represent one of the most important factors in determining which career or job you choose. If you ignore what you value in work and life, you set yourself up for disappointment and failure. Values motivate you. Values predict your success in a job. Values, in essence, determine which jobs are right for you.

TRUE STORY

When the Job Doesn't Fit the Values

Rob is a 36-year-old married man and father of two. He works for a large municipal telephone company, installing corporate phone systems. He receives his job orders from a cranky, demanding supervisor. Rob hates his job. He makes use of every vacation and sick day, and he is constantly grumbling about his awful work. He doesn't like to get up in the morning and is depressed on Sunday nights. After completing self-assessment exercises, Rob discovered that his values are **Adventure, Independence, Creativity, Change,** and **Variety.**

Is it any wonder Rob is miserable? His present job allows for none of his values to be realized. His need for adventure, independence, and creativity isn't met at the telephone company. He needs to change careers or increase his leisure activities to include these values. If he doesn't, happiness and success will be lost to him. He's already lost too many years in a career that isn't a good match for him.

The Exercise

The *Guide for Occupational Exploration* describes a variety of values that motivate people. Check off from the following list those values that are most important to you. Then go back and choose five, rating them with the most important one first. If you find that two values are of equal importance, choose between them as best you can and put that ahead of the other.

_____ **Security:** the assurance of not losing my job

_____ **Stability:** maintaining steady workloads and job responsibilities that are unlikely to change

_____ **Financial Gain:** the opportunity to make a lot of money

_____ **Competition:** an environment where I can challenge my abilities against others

_____ **Recognition:** public acknowledgment for a job well done

_____ **Prestige:** a job or career that carries with it a lot of admiration or envy

_____ **Independence:** the ability to work on my own and make my own decisions

_____ **Precision Work:** working on projects that require extensive attention to detail with little room for mistakes

_____ **Supervision:** directly overseeing the work of others

_____ **Influence People:** changing or influencing others

_____ **Power and Authority:** controlling the work and career paths of others

_____ **Work Under Pressure:** demanding work in which my performance can be judged by others

_____ **Make Decisions:** opportunities to influence the decision-making process within an organization

_____ **Public Contact:** be in the company of others on a daily basis

_____ **Work With Others:** be part of a team working toward specific goals

_____ **Work Alone:** work on projects by myself

_____ **Knowledge:** be in an environment where I can find the information needed to solve problems and reach goals

_____ **Change and Variety:** having responsibilities that regularly change in their content and type of challenge

_____ **Physical Challenge:** using physical attributes in a demanding, rewarding environment

_____ **Help Society:** be able to improve the lives of others

_____ **Affiliation:** be known for my belonging to a particular organization

_____ **Friendships:** developing personal relationships with coworkers

_____ **Intellectual Status:** be regarded as knowledgeable and an expert within my field

_____ **Creativity:** develop new programs, ideas, or products in a way not thought of before

_____ **Aesthetics:** the ability to appreciate and experience the beauty of things

_____ **Excitement:** experience or engage in exciting activities

_____ **Adventure:** engage in risk-taking experiences

_____ **Family:** have the freedom to enjoy my family without the responsibilities of work interfering

_____ **Moral Fulfillment:** a job where I can contribute to advancing ethical and moral values

_____ **Location:** working in a particular town, city, or region that complements my lifestyle

_____ **Community:** participate in the activities of the larger community

_____ **Travel:** a job that allows me to engage in a fair amount of traveling

_____ **Leisure:** having enough time to engage in personal, pleasurable activities

The Results

List in order of importance the five values you have checked off that best describe your needs:

1. _____

2. _____

3. _____

4. _____

5. _____

Questions to Consider

1. Of the values I checked, which one(s) _must_ be present in order for me to be happy in a job?

2. Are any of the values I chose present in the job or career I am now seeking?

3. Is there anyone I know whose values contradict the job that they presently hold? Do I think they're happy or frustrated with their work?

4. Do any of my leisure activities enable me to use and/or express these values? (If not, or not enough, then think of ways in which you can better incorporate more of these values in your leisure time, through sports, hobbies, volunteerism, or religious or social activities.

IN SHORT

After completing all the exercises in this chapter, you should be able to answer the questions below:

My three most important interests are:

1. _____

2. _____

3. _____

My three greatest skills and abilities are:

1. _____

2. _____

3. _____

My five most important values are:

1. _____

2. _____

3. _____

4. _____

5. _____

You might be saying to yourself, "So, I've completed the self-assessment exercises, now what? What do my interests, skills and values have to do with choosing a career?" The next chapter will show you how to go about analyzing your results and choosing a career.

CHAPTER | 2

In the last chapter you discovered three crucial things about yourself: the three interests that are most important to you, your three greatest strengths, and your five most important values. In this chapter, you will see how all of these can be used to help you choose your career.

EXPLORING CAREERS
MAKING THE RIGHT MATCH

What makes *you* fit into a particular role? What unique combination of talents and abilities makes *you* "the right type" for a specific job? Or, like Michael in the box, "The Wrong Fit" (seee next page), can you make yourself different? Can you redesign yourself to fit into almost any job or career that happens to be available at the moment?

If you're like most people, your answer is "no." Your unique experiences and abilities determine who you are. Therefore you must know *who* you are and what careers would be best suited to you, if you are to convince someone else—an employer—than you're right for the job.

TRUE STORY

The Wrong Fit

There is a scene in the movie *Tootsie* where Dustin Hoffman, auditioning for a role in a play, is interrupted by the director, who says: "I'm sorry Michael, you're just the wrong type."

"Oh, I can be taller", Michael replies.

"No, no, you don't understand," says the director. "We're looking for somebody shorter."

"Oh, well, look, I don't have to be this tall. I'm wearing lifts. I can be *shorter*," explains Michael.

In exasperation, the director responds: "I know, but we're looking for somebody different."

"I can be different!"

Then, in a voice filled with disgust, the director says: "We're looking for somebody *else,* OK?"

SEVEN STEPS IN CAREER DECISION-MAKING

There are seven major steps to take in choosing the career that is best for you. Each step is important, and it's best to complete them in the order here. One step builds on the next, until you have come to the point of actually choosing your career.

1. **Complete the exercises in Chapter 1.** This will help you to see for yourself which are your most significant skills, interests, and values.

2. **Consider two or three careers that interest you.** Base your choices on your past experience, what you like to do, or what you always wished you could do. If you have no idea what careers are available to you, the following sources, which can be found in local libraries and bookstores, can provide you with many options:

     a. *America's Top Jobs for People Without College Degrees*, by J. Michael Farr, contains a wonderful "Job Matching Chart."

This chart contains 200 jobs (which cover over 80 percent of the labor force), arranged into related groups or clusters. An example of a cluster is "Communication, Visual Arts, and Performing Arts Occupations." Under the section "Visual Arts" are the job titles: Designers, Photographers, and Visual Artists. Each job title is identified by the skills and interests associated with it, the working conditions, the education and training required, and the employment outlook and earning potential. This is a very easy-to-read, concise method of discovering potential careers based on your self-assessment results. It will describe careers that you might never have thought to consider.

b. *Careers for the '90's*, published by the Research and Education Association, is a comprehensive handbook that describes over 250 careers. Each career is listed under an Occupational Cluster, so it's easy to research. The information covers earnings, required education, working conditions, and outlook for the future.

3. **Talk to someone in each of the career fields you have chosen to research.** For instance, if you are interested in becoming a chef, go to one of your favorite restaurants. Explain to the maitre d' that you are involved in a career research project. Then ask if you can interview the chef. There is no substitute for talking to someone who is working in the field. The information you gain will be enormously beneficial in making a decision.

4. **Spend a day in their shoes.** You can follow someone as she performs her job. You can also volunteer in the field to get a true taste of what the job is all about.

5. **Go to the library.** Ask for the *Occupational Outlook Handbook*, as well as some of the other excellent resources that you'll find in Additional Resources at the end of this book. Read up on the careers you've singled out and gather information on each:
   - employment outlook
   - nature of the work
   - requirements and training
   - earning potential
   - skills required

6. **Review your research.** Talk over your options with someone you trust. Look objectively at each career in terms of how well it matches your skills, interests, and values. To help you do this, complete the sample checklist at the end of this chapter.

7. **Make a decision and follow through!** If the career you ultimately select requires that you get additional training or education, use your researching abilities to locate an appropriate school or program. Refer to "Education and Training for Careers" in Additional Resources at the end of this book. If you've got what it takes to get into your chosen career right now, then the rest of this book will lead you through the job search process.

A CASE HISTORY
Career Decision-Making in Action

Angela, an 18-year-old high school graduate, was unable to make a decision about whether to enroll in college or go out and get a full-time job. She had always enjoyed helping others, especially children. She was a youth group leader in her church, she tutored elementary school children while in high school, and she was leader of the local chapter of Students Against Drunk Driving.

Her mother worked as a legal secretary in a large corporate law firm. She told Angela that she could arrange for a full-time secretarial job for her in the word processing department that would come with a good salary and full benefits. Her mother thought she'd be foolish to pass up such an opportunity.

SELF-ASSESSMENT

Angela knew that she first needed to explore her strengths and interests, and the things that she valued in work. She completed the self-assessment exercises in chapter 1 and discovered that:

- Her three most important interests are humanitarian, leading and influencing, and accommodating
- Her three greatest strengths are social, working with others, and verbal
- Her five most important values are help society, moral fulfillment, public contact, community, and friendships

CONDUCTING RESEARCH

Angela decided to do a little research about several different careers. Since she always enjoyed helping children, she decided to find out about a career in teaching. At the same time, she would look into a career as a legal secretary.

Talking to Professionals About Their Jobs

First, Angela visited with her cousin Rhoda, who was an elementary school teacher. She asked Rhoda what she liked about teaching and what she didn't like. Angela asked about the requirements Rhoda had to meet to become a teacher, how hard it was to get a job, and what the salary range was. Would she recommend the career for Angela? Angela listened and took notes.

Next, Angela decided to go to work with her mother for a day. She spent the entire day watching and taking notes, learning exactly what a legal secretary does. She sat with her mother as she took stenography. She accompanied her to the mail room and reprographic department. She watched her mother prepare a 12-page legal brief. She listened as her mother expertly managed the telephone and watched as she made visitors feel welcome.

Making Friends with the Local Librarian

The local library was the next step in Angela's fact-seeking mission. She asked the librarian for the *Occupational Outlook Handbook,* which is updated each year and published by the U.S. Department of Labor. Since this is a reference book, Angela could not check it out, but she had brought a pad and pen for notes and change for the copy machine. She looked under the table of contents and found a category titled, "**Teachers, Librarians, and Counselors.**" In that section she turned to the subheading, "**School Teachers: Kindergarten, Elementary, and Secondary.**" There she hit pay dirt: six pages of very good information about being an elementary school teacher.

She discovered exactly what teachers do, how they do it, whom they work with, working conditions, qualifications and educational requirements, job outlook and earning potential, and a section titled, "**Sources of Additional Information.**"

Next, she went back to the table of contents and under the category, "**Administrative, Support Occupations, Including Clerical,**" she found the subheading, "**Secretaries.**" She made copies of both of the sections, on elementary teacher and secretary.

EVALUATING AND SYNTHESIZING THE INFORMATION

Now Angela was ready to review her research and make the decision either to enroll in college to get her teaching degree or to accept the secretarial job with her mother's law firm.

Matching the Job with the Person

As she read the notes she'd taken and the pages she'd copied, Angela found out that secretaries spend a lot of their time typing, particularly at a computer terminal, and spend long periods of time sitting. They have some contact with clients, but it is usually minimal. In general, secretaries perform and coordinate office activities and insure that information gets disseminated to staff and clients. There would be little opportunity for Angela's greatest interests (humanitarian, leading, and influencing) to be utilized. And there would be little likelihood that her strongest values (help society, moral fulfillment, and community) will be realized.

She saw that there was a much better match between her interests, values, and strengths and a career in teaching. She knows that teachers play a vital role in the development of children, introducing them to numbers, language, science, and social studies. Seeing students develop new skills and instilling in them the love of learning is a very rewarding job.

Angela's research showed that the entry-level salary of an elementary teacher is about equal to that of a secretary. But to become a teacher she would have to go to college for four years to obtain a bachelor's degree, and she would eventually need a master's. For the secretarial job, she'd need no further training; her present level of computer and interpersonal skills are all she would need for now.

The job outlook for both careers was very positive. Angela already knew that there was a job waiting for her in her mother's law firm. Also, Angela's cousin Rhoda told her that there was a shortage of elementary school teachers in her district and probably would be for some years.

Using a Checklist to Evaluate Your Options

With all this information in mind, Angela made a decision. She prepared a checklist of the most important factors that had an influence on her decision and added them up to see which career would make the best match.

Angela's Checklist

	Secretary	Teacher
Type of work I find most rewarding		X
Meets my values		X
Utilizes my skills and abilities		X
Matches my interests with job requirements		X
Easy entry into career	X	
Employment outlook	X	X
Salary	X	X
Total	3	6

It was clear to Angela that she'd be happier and probably more successful as a teacher. Since she knew that she could go to college and probably wouldn't have a problem getting her degree, this was the best choice for her. Angela entered college that fall, and during the summer she worked as a temporary secretary in her mother's law firm to make extra money for her tuition.

MORE DECISIONS AHEAD

Like Angela, you will make a good career decision if you take the time to gather the information you need and then compare your options objectively. Use the blank checklist at the end of this chapter to decide which career would be your best match.

Keep in mind, though, that the decision you make right now is appropriate for you *today,* but your needs and values will change as you grow in years and experience. You'll be faced with many more decisions about your job and your career path as you go. Sometimes it may be due to outside factors, like a company about to downsize or relocate. Other times you will be making decisions because of your own needs. Perhaps you'll want to make a mid-life career change or feel it's time to move up and advance. Whatever the reason, you will find that the research and decision-making process you used to get this far will serve you well again.

Knowing who you are—what your strengths are and what matters most to you in life—will enable you to handle each decision and each career move with wisdom and purpose.

IN SHORT

This chapter showed you how to do the following steps in the career decision-making process:

- Evaluate your self-assessment results
- Conduct research by talking to professionals and getting help from your local librarian
- Evaluate and synthesize all your information
- Match job "personalities" with your personality
- Use a checklist to evaluate your alternatives
- Choose a career that's right for you!

Once you've decided upon a career and have the skills and education you need to get started in that career, you're ready to move on. The next step is to explore the job market and begin to target your search on those fields and types of employers that hold the most promise. This is just what Chapter 3 is all about.

CHECKLIST
(Complete one for each career you research)

	Yes	No
Is this the kind of work I would find rewarding?	_____	_____
Does it meet my values?	_____	_____
Does it utilize my skills and abilities?	_____	_____
Do the job requirements match my interests?	_____	_____
Does the nature of the work interest me?	_____	_____
Is there a positive employment outlook?	_____	_____
Is the salary range adequate for my needs?	_____	_____
Can I meet the training/educational requirements?	_____	_____
Do I find the working conditions favorable?	_____	_____
Are the related occupations interesting to me?	_____	_____
Have I researched all the sources available to be sure I have sufficient and up-to-date information?	_____	_____
Total	_____	_____

CHAPTER | 3

Now that you know your strongest interests, skills, and values and what type of work you want to do, the question is: *Where do you want to do it?* This chapter will help you target the industries that will best suit you.

WHERE DO YOU WANT TO WORK?
TARGETING YOUR INDUSTRY

The job you hope to be doing in the near future will be very much affected by where you do it. The field you work in and the type and size of the company or organization can play a very big role in your work success and sense of satisfaction. Where you work will determine the types of people you spend your working hours with, perhaps even your job security and opportunities for advancement.

DEFINING THE FACTORS

For most professions, there are several different industries where that particular type of work can be performed. For instance, accountants work in banking, government, or private corporations, or else they are self-employed. Counselors work in city agencies, colleges, private or public schools, hospitals, or insurance companies. Even librarians have choices. They work in colleges, public and private libraries, school library media centers, law firms, or publishing houses.

The choice of which industry you want to work in is influenced by a number of factors:

- The population you wish to serve
- The work environment in which you're most comfortable
- The types of people you want to work with (your coworkers)
- Your goals
- Entry requirements
- Your values
- Market conditions
- Geographic limitations

The Population You Wish to Serve

Whether your clients are corporate business leaders or the homeless, you must understand their needs, as well as your own, before making a choice.

When thinking about the kind of people you would like to serve (in other words, your clients), you need to think about what you value in work. If you value helping society and seek moral fulfillment, but you accept a position where your only contact with the a client is an occasional E-mail to a person you never met, think twice. This job is probably not for you.

Take a look at Emanuel, in the box "Keeping His Real Goal in Focus," and how he made a career decision based on the population with which he wanted to work.

TRUE STORY

Keeping His Real Goal in Focus

Emanuel graduated in the top 10 percent of his law school class. He was approached by a recruiter for Kravatz and Sloane, one of the largest corporate law firms in the city. They offered him a competitive salary with attractive benefits. His clients would be national corporations needing legal advice on contracts and mergers.

Emanuel grew up in the poor section of town, and always wanted to give something back to his community. Despite the lure of money and prestige, Emanuel decided to turn down the law firm's offer and accept a position in the city government's legal aid division, where his clients would require legal assistance on a broad base of issues. Emanuel would be working with the people he most wanted to help, and he'd be learning a great deal about many different aspects of law.

The Environment

Think about the type of workplace in which you would be most happy and productive:

- Do you like fast-paced action—or do you prefer a slower, more relaxed work pace?
- Do you like to work in an office environment—or do you need to be out on the road?
- Do you like a formal corporate culture—or would you be happier in a casual, let-your-hair-down atmosphere?

The type of environment you work in will have a definite impact on your success. After all, you can't rise through the ranks of a company if you are always wearing khakis and sweaters and your bosses are all in three-piece business suits.

Most people, even at a very young age, know the kind of environment in which they're most comfortable and in which they can thrive. Think about your interests and where you're most yourself. Later on in this chapter, you'll discover ways to learn about the work environments most common for the industry you are considering.

The People You Work With

According to the Strong Interest Inventory, a popular career assessment test (Consulting Psychologists Press, Inc.), people in particular careers share a common interest pattern. In other words, most counselors would have a strikingly similar pattern of occupational, educational, and personal preferences. For instance, the majority of counselors who take the test report that they like working with outspoken people, high school students, and physically disabled people. They enjoy jazz or rock concerts, art galleries, and skiing.

It's difficult to say what things in our lives influence our likes and dislikes. However, it is clear that if most people in a particular career share common likes and dislikes, it's important that you pay attention to them. If the majority of your coworkers like working outdoors, using their hands, and preferring little supervision, but you like working at a desk, using a computer, and having clear authority figures, it's time to change jobs.

Your Goals

It's important to have some idea as to where you see yourself in the next five years. Your choice of industry will depend on that vision.

Let's say you just graduated from college with a bachelor's degree in marketing. You want to start a career in advertising sales for the local newspaper. You see yourself staying in sales for about four years and then moving into management.

After two years you realize that the only salespeople to be promoted are those who pursue their MBAs. You never intended to go back to school, and you become disillusioned. You think about your roommate from college who took a position as a salesperson at a local radio station. He was just promoted to Assistant Manager. While your friend attained his career goals in a different industry, clearly, you will not be able to attain yours in the time frame you originally planned.

Clarifying your goals and researching the industry are essential steps towards career fulfillment.

Entry Requirements

Different industries require different qualifications for the same job title. For instance, accountants who work in one of the big six accounting firms are required to obtain CPA licenses within a year of employment. However, accountants who work in government need never apply for that license.

You must decide if the entry requirements for a particular industry are feasible and agreeable to you. Otherwise, you need to look elsewhere.

TRUE STORY

Knowing What Makes You Happy

Jill completed a three-month certificate program as a nurse's aide and at first was delighted when she found a position in a large metropolitan hospital. Jill was only one of two aides on a post-surgical floor with thirty-two patients. The hospital was in the process of downsizing. Despite the fact that she was overworked and overwhelmed, Jill was told how lucky she was just to have a job.

It didn't take Jill long to realize that she really wasn't so lucky. The reason she went into the field in the first place was because she felt a strong moral duty to help others, a strong need to make a difference in the community, and a desire to influence people on an individual basis. At the hospital, she was stretched so thin and stressed so badly that she was unable to help anyone. She felt inadequate and frustrated all the time.

Jill's aunt told her about an opening in a nearby nursing home. Jill applied for and was offered the position. Instead of thirty-two patients, she now has twelve residents to care for. She provides basic care and companionship to people with whom she can build a relationship. For the first time, Jill feels fulfilled and secure in her career decision.

As you can see, Jill found a job that met her educational and career objectives, yet she was unhappy. It came down to a job and an industry that did not meet her values. Once she was able to fulfill her need to help others and make a difference in her community, success and happiness followed.

Meeting Your Values

In Chapter 2 you identified your five most important values. Remember, values represent those factors that need to be present in your job if you are to be happy and motivated. Jill's story illustrates the importance of considering your values in choosing an industry.

Market Conditions

It's possible that you have done all the research. You know the population you wish to serve, the kinds of people you want to work with, your long and short-range goals, the entry requirements, and how your values fit into the industry. However, if you have ignored the market condition of that particular industry, you could have completely wasted your time.

The market condition measures the health of the industry you have chosen. If you made plans to enter the public school system, but failed to discover that they were on a three-year hiring freeze, you lose. If you decided to build a career in finance, but ignored the bottoming out of the banking industry and the laying off of employees, you lose.

Be a winner; research the market.

Geographic Limitations

We are all bound by the environments in which we live. If we live in an urban community, our options (barring agricultural jobs) are almost limitless. But if we live in a rural community, our options are much fewer.

When choosing a field to enter, be well aware of your options. Consider whether you are willing to relocate to another city, state, or country. If you are, you can open yourself up to almost any opportunity. Your options are unlimited. You can target *any* industry that appeals to you. You will not have any of the restraints of remaining within the opportunities of your own community.

However, if you decide to find a job in the area you now live, you will need to discover the industries that are located within a reasonable distance from your home. Know just how far you are willing to travel to enter your chosen field. A good idea is to draw an imaginary line around the perimeters of how far you want to travel, and only seek out those industries that fall within that line.

RESEARCHING THE INDUSTRY

Now that you know the important things to consider in choosing a job market, you are about to discover the resources available that will assist you in gathering information. Check out Additional Resources at the end of this book for details on the books and magazines mentioned below.

Newspapers

No matter what career or job market you intend to pursue, it is extremely important that you read the news on a daily basis. The best way to discover job trends, shrinking markets, new directions, and future opportunities is to read the paper. If you have a computer and enjoy going online, you'll be happy to know that most major newspapers throughout the country are available on the Internet.

Other Publications

Magazines, like *Business Week* and *Forbes*, and trade journals, such as *Publishers Weekly, Advertising Age*, and *Supermarket News*, offer current business news and analysis on a more focused level than newspapers. The articles offer in-depth coverage of both global and national market economies, as well as analysis of industry sectors and individual businesses.

Career Handbooks

In Chapter 2, Career Exploration, you read about *Occupational Outlook Handbook*. Mostly all the factors that influence your choice of industry can be found for each of the 250–300 careers highlighted in this book. It describes earnings growth projections, training requirements in particular industries, client populations, labor market trends, entry requirements, and working environments.

EVALUATION AND DECISION-MAKING

Once you have gathered information on all the factors for each industry, you will need to evaluate the material and make a decision. First, take a look at Jamie and how he evaluated industry information to make a career decision. Later on, you will follow the same steps to make *your own* career decision.

CASE HISTORY—JAMIE

Jamie, a 22 year old high school graduate, had just completed a Heating, Air-Conditioning, and Refrigeration Technician training program. He was contemplating three job offers: one in a local hospital, one in a private construction company, and the other in a large corporate office building downtown. His goal was to accept an entry-level position, and then either move into a supervisory position, or open his own contracting business. His values were family, location, knowledge, supervision, and working with others.

He researched each industry using a number of the sources above. The charts on the next page illustrate the information he gathered, his evaluation of the material, and his final decision.

In his Chart A Jamie listed the key work factors down the left-hand side and then described them for all three of his job options. In Chart B Jamie evaluated the three positions based on these key factors. As you can see, two of his choices, the hospital position and the corporate one, had the same number of favorable factors. However, the position in the corporate office building had a much better market condition. The job was stable, and Jamie didn't have to worry about being downsized in six months. Jamie was engaged and planned on getting married and starting a family in three years, so he needed to have a secure start to his career.

The factors *most* important to him were: market condition, meeting his values, type of work environment, and population he would serve. Since the corporate job best met these factors, his choice was clear to him; he took the position in the corporate office building downtown.

CHARTING YOUR CHOICES

Use your blank Chart A at the end of this chapter to record all information you have amassed for each industry you researched. Then, in your Chart B, place a check mark under each factor that is favorable to your needs and interests. Evaluate the information, comparing each factor within each industry just as Jamie did. Choose the industry that provides the best match.

Jamie's CHART A
Job Title: Heating, Air Conditioning, and Refrigeration Technician

Factors	Hospital (Industry 1)	Construction (Industry 2)	Corporate Office (Industry 3)
Population	Hospital staff, patients	Little interaction with clients	Corporate employees of varying levels
Type of Work	Maintenance & repair	Installation of new units	Maintenance & repair
Environment	Semi-professional	Casual	Professional
Coworkers	Older, learned trade on the job, union	Younger, like new challenges, seek adventure & independence	Licensed & formally trained, family oriented
Goals	Ability to rise to management within 5 years	Ability to network & open own business within 10 years	Ability to be promoted after 5 years
Entry Requirements	One year technical school	18-month apprenticeship program	One year technical school & certification
Meeting values	Location, Family, potential supervision	Knowledge, potential supervision	Working with others, potential supervision
Market Conditions	Downsizing all hospital workers	Seasonal, new housing up 3% this month	Stable
Geographic Limitations	Local	Travel house-to-house	Commute

CHART B

	Population	Type of Work	Environment	Coworkers	Goals	Entry Requirements	Values	Market	Geographic Locations
Hospitals		X	X		X	X	X		X
Construction				X					
Corporate	X	X	X			X	X	X	

IN SHORT

The best decision you can make in choosing your career and the industry you will work in is an *informed* one. It's a decision based on self-knowledge, career information, and market trends. It's a decision that will lead you towards success and well-being. You are surely on your way now!

The remaining chapters are devoted to the tools and techniques you need to develop to find the job that, until now, you only dreamed about.

Use this blank chart to describe your industry options in terms of key work factors, just as Jamie did.

CHART A			
Factors	**(Industry 1)**	**(Industry 2)**	**(Industry 3)**
Population			
Type of Work			
Environment			
Coworkers			
Goals			
Entry Requirements			
Meeting values			
Market			
Conditions			
Geographic Limitations			

CHART B	Population	Type of Work	Environment	Coworkers	Goals	Entry Requirements	Values	Market	Geographic Locations
Industry 1									
Industry 2									
Industry 3									

My ideal industry:

CHAPTER | 4

A resume is the first tool, and one of the most important ones, in the job search process. This chapter describes four types of resumes and how they are used, so you can choose a style to meet your specific needs.

RESUME TYPES
CHOOSE THE ONE THAT WILL WORK FOR YOU

A resume is a brief summary of your professional background. It is not a long, inclusive history of everything you ever did and every school you ever attended. Rather, it presents your skills and work history in a clear, concise format that's attractive and easy to read.

A resume does not get you a job. It gets you an interview. Your sole objective in writing a resume is to get you through the door. When an employer advertises for a position and receives fifty resumes and cover letters, his job is to screen out undesirable candidates and then choose a small number of ones that show the most promise and seem especially suited to the job. Most busy employers do not have the time to wade through long and complicated resumes. They've got about 30 seconds, on average, to review each one. Your challenge is to effectively present yourself in a resume so that you don't get put in the reject pile.

A GOOD RESUME

What makes for a winning resume? Its presentation is:

- Concise and to the point
- Clear in language and format
- Easy to read
- Free of spelling and grammar mistakes
- One full page only
- Professional looking, printed on quality paper

And in content it:

- Is geared to the job available
- Meets the employer's needs
- Promotes you and your background in a positive manner
- Contains relevant job and education history

In addition, a good resume is packed with key words that describe your experience and skills in the language employers expect. To get a good sense of this language, peruse the want ads to see what these words are. After all, that's where employers say what they're looking for.

Use "administrative assistant" rather than "secretary," "internship" rather than "summer job," "self-starter" instead of "works well alone." A few minutes with the want ads will show you the hot words in your field.

A POOR RESUME

When deciding what to include in your resume, always ask yourself the question, "Do these words help describe me and what I can do for the job in a positive way?" Never put negative information in your resume. One job seeker asked if including her former high school, the years she attended, and "Never Graduated" could be construed as negative. It certainly could! Simply including the dates she attended high school would be better.

According to Richard Beatty in his book, *The Resume Kit,* the following "knockout" factors signal the employer to stop reading and move on to the next resume:

- job objective is incompatible with current openings
- inadequate educational credentials
- poorly organized, sloppy or hard to read
- too many employers in too short a period of time
- too many pages

TYPES OF RESUMES

There are four major types of resumes:

1. Chronological
2. Functional or Skills
3. Linear
4. Electronic

An example of each kind appears at the end of this chapter.

THE CHRONOLOGICAL RESUME

The chronological resume is, by far, the most common. It is called a chronological resume because it highlights your employment and educational history by date and year. It shows the progression of your career in an easy-to-read format.

Description

The format is easy to follow, and since you are preparing your resume yourself, this is important. After your heading (your name and contact information) the resume begins with an Objective, most often followed by Work Experience (presented in reverse chronological order, with your most recent job first). Then comes Education, also organized in reverse chronological order.(If you don't have a lot of Experience, you may want to put Education first.) Then come Skills and/or Interests.

If you have any gaps in your work history, you might have a problem with this format. Clearly, if you are highlighting your dates of employment, the gap is sure to be apparent. And employment gaps signal negative reactions in employers. For instance: Was this person fired from a previous job and unable to find work? Is this person lazy and unmotivated?

Did this person have some sort of chronic illness that kept her out of work? While it is possible that none of these factors apply to you, the employer is bound to think them. If you have any gaps in your work history, Chapter 6 will offer suggestions on how to deal with them.

Another possible shortcoming in using the chronological resume is having little or no job experience. Many novice job seekers ask, "How can I fill up an Experience section if I have no experience?" If this might be your question, don't automatically dismiss this type of resume. Look at the sample chronological resume at the end of this chapter. You'll also find some helpful suggestions for getting around this problem in Chapter 6.

Purpose

Chronological resumes are used by most entry-level workers. Why does it work so well? Because the employer can *quickly* scan the resume, observing where and when you worked and went to school. Your job responsibilities are clearly written and easily accessible to the employer.

The chronological format is the one that works best for most entry-level job hunters, and it's the one you should use when preparing your own resume, unless you're certain one of the other formats presents you in a better light. Not only is it easy to read and prepare, it also offers the best means of showing entry-level experience. Besides, most employers prefer it. There's a logical, easy-to-read flow from one employer to another, and it highlights continuity of employment and career, both of which are viewed favorably by employers.

THE FUNCTIONAL/SKILLS RESUME

As its title suggests, this resume format highlights the skills you have amassed in your career, not the particular jobs you have held. Your employers are mentioned only at the end of your resume.

Description

A functional or skills resume is not as easily reviewed by employers as chronological resumes. This is because its format makes it more difficult to figure out how long you were at a job, and where you learned and performed each skill. You are at a disadvantage if the employer doesn't have the extra time it takes to read through such a resume. Also, it's a more difficult type of resume to write. You must first translate all your experience into four or five broad skills groupings. Then, you need to decide in which category each skill belongs.

Purpose

This is a good format for people who have:

- Risen high in the corporate ladder and have broad groupings of skills
- Had many jobs and want to focus on *what* they did as opposed to *where* they did it
- Learned a necessary skill for a particular job, but did not spend a lot of time using it in their career
- Had several different careers and job responsibilities
- Have gaps in their career

THE LINEAR RESUME

Very similar to the chronological resume, the linear resume presents education and work history in a chronological format.

Description

The two major differences are:

1. Instead of an Objective, the linear resume has a Professional Profile. Professional profiles summarize the job seeker's career in three to four sentences. Information you would include in a professional profile would be the:
   - Number of years you spent in the career
   - Field you specialize in
   - Strongest skills you possess
   - Goals for your future position

2. A brief summary (two to three lines) would follow your job title for each job you held. Rather than focusing on the particular tasks a job seeker performed, the summary lets the employer know who the job seeker was within that organization.

Purpose

As you may have surmised, this resume best serves the more experienced job seeker. It's an ideal format for someone with years of expertise and experience. It's a great way to highlight major accomplishments without losing the clear, concise format of the chronological resume.

THE ELECTRONIC RESUME

The electronic resume may very well be the wave of the future. According to the U.S. Department of Labor, most large companies and 40 percent of midsize ones are now relying on resume scanning software to screen in-coming resumes. Scanning has become popular because the technology is readily available, and also because Human Resource departments have been cut back and there are larger numbers of applicants than ever before to screen.

Description

As you can see from the sample electronic resume at the end of the chapter, this type begins with a list of keywords. Anticipate the keywords an employer will attach to the position you seek by keeping a log of words taken from help wanted ads and other sources. Electronic resume software programs search for job titles, departments, degrees, universities attended, companies worked for, and the organizations you belong to. Try to use the keywords as often as possible, without "overburdening" your resume with them.

After the keywords comes a list of Skills, again using the keywords. Then comes Employment History, Education, and any other important information.

Have plenty of white space in your resume. As a new job seeker, you should keep your resume to one page. Use a high-quality printer, but don't use fancy typefaces—the plainer, the better. Be careful of using small o's as bullets; the computer may read them as the letter "O." *Italics*, underlining, and shadowing look nice, but they will totally confuse the scanner. If you must be stylistic, stick to **bold** type only.

Purpose

When a position becomes available, the scanning software directs the computer to search resumes for specific keywords pertaining to that position. Applicants who submit their resumes with the most number of matching keywords (they must match exactly) will be considered for interviews.

You should use this type of resume as a supplement (not substitute) for a more traditional style. Although the job market is constantly changing, traditional methods of job seeking still prevail.

IN SHORT

There are four main resume types:
- Chronological
- Function/skills
- Linear
- Electronic

The chronological resume is the most popular, is the best type for you to use. It's easy to write, and it's easy to read, which is especially important with employers who often have to pore over dozens of resumes at a time. It also does the best job of highlighting entry-level experience.

To see how this works, review the sample resumes that follow. Then get ready to gather the information you'll need to write your resume.

ROBERT L. D'ANGELO
3957 Hazelwood Court
Washington, D.C. 20032
(202) 459-9232

OBJECTIVE: *An entry level x-ray technologist position in a health care facility where I can utilize my training and education*

EDUCATION:
1995-Present

Baltimore Community College, Baltimore, MD
A.A.S.-*X-Ray Technologist Program*
Degree expected 9/97

1994

Hamden Training Institute, Washington, D.C.
Certificate in WordPerfect 5.0 and
Lotus 1-2-3

**VOLUNTEER
EXPERIENCE:**
1996-Present

Chelsea Street Clinic, Baltimore, MD
Intern
• Assisted staff in the X-ray department in preparing and processing patient X-rays
• Filed patient data into computer system
• Interacted with patients in a courteous, helpful manner
• Interviewed patients regarding their personal and medical history

EXPERIENCE:
1993-1995

Miggy's Restaurant, Washington, D.C.
Busboy
• Maintained the cleanliness of all tables and linen
• Set tables with clean linen and silverware
• Assisted with washing and disinfecting dishes and glassware
• Provided general clean up of restaurant after hours

**COMMUNITY
INVOLVEMENT:**

St. Simeon's Church, Washington, D.C. 1991-1993
Assisted youth group during recreational outings and group meetings

SKILLS:

Fluent in Italian
Basic knowledge of computer, including WordPerfect 6.0 and Lotus 1-2-3

REFERENCES: Furnished upon request

MARY ELLEN MCDERMOTT
25 Heathrow Lane
Albany, New York 00323
(518) 934-3290

PROFESSIONAL PROFILE: Multifaceted professional with twenty years experience, utilizing highly developed technical, management, and instructional skills. Extremely motivated, self-starter seeking career diversity.

SKILLS
Medical Technology
- Experienced in techniques in varied types of chemistry labs, including organic and inorganic, industrial and hospital settings.
- Medical technician and weekend supervisor for clinical chemistry lab in a 1,000-bed teaching hospital.
- Knowledge of every phase of clinical chemistry, both manually and operationally.
- Directed the daily operation of a Boston clinic hematology lab, including routine CBC's and blood drawing.

Research
- Studied, tested and developed new antibiotics for kidney specialist in infectious diseases.
- Performed kidney surgery on laboratory animals, running tests on kidney function after surgery.
- Organized data for doctor and authored research papers.

Management
- Managed entire clinical chemistry lab with a staff of 25 medical technicians, generating computer reports and trouble-shooting machinery.
- Organized the daily operation of a new retail store, responsible for buying, hiring, and supervising staff of six.
- Created new lines of merchandise, establishing productive and long-standing relationships with wholesalers.

Teaching
- Instructed medical technician students during their clinical internship in clinical chemistry procedures.
- Instructor for grades K-5 in various subjects, including creative writing, music, and social studies

EMPLOYMENT HISTORY
3/93–Present   ALBANY BOARD OF EDUCATION Albany, New York
Teacher

7/86–9/91   CONTEMPORARY OFFICE STAFF Boston, Massachusetts
Assistant Manager

4/77–10/84   BOSTON GENERAL HOSPITAL Boston, Massachusetts
Medical Technologist

EDUCATION
BOSTON UNIVERSITY Boston, Massachusetts
B.S. in Chemistry
Dean's List, Four Years

REFERENCES: Furnished upon request.

Sample of Functional Resume

RITA EDGEWATER
1456 Elm Park
Atlanta, Georgia 32505
(404) 432-5393

PROFESSIONAL PROFILE: *Over nine years professional experience in education and job training, offering expertise in counseling, program development, and workshop facilitation, in higher education and adult training arenas*

EXERIENCE

1994–Present **Adult Training Institute,** Atlanta, GA
Job Developer/Case Manager
Provided wide range of counseling and job development activities for dislocated workers, including one-on-one and group counseling, corporate networking, and workshop development
- Manage job development/job placement activities for all participants
- Conduct workshops in job readiness and job search skills
- Research labor market strategies
- Prepare schedules for workshops, orientation, and assessment
- Make appropriate referrals to outside agencies

1992–1994 **Georgia Tech., Nurse Aide Training Program,** Atlanta, GA
Counselor/Job Developer
Provided all facets of support for low-income women in a job training program, including community outreach, counseling, and job development
- Counseled and supported students in all aspects of training
- Developed and organized weekly workshops in job readiness and job search skills
- Performed all job development/job placement activities
- Coordinated programs with Department of Labor

1988–1992 **Georgia Tech.,** Atlanta, GA
Coordinator of GED Program
Developed, administered, and coordinated GED program for adult student population, including preparing budgets, final reports, and grants in a Department-wide refunding effort
- GED Instructor for class of 18 students
- Increased enrollment and funding by 25%
- Selected teachers, materials, curriculum, staffp; program development

EDUCATION HISTORY
Georgia Tech.
B.A. in Social Work   Cumulative G.P.A. **3.93,** Major **4.0**

PROFESSIONAL AFFILIATIONS
1994–Present   Associate Member—Atlanta Economic Development Corp.
1989–Present   Advisory Board—Halloran Halfway House
1986–1987   Advisory Board—President's Committee for the Disabled

REFERENCES: Furnished upon request

Sample Linear Resume

44

AGNES MILLHOUSE
82 University Place
Detroit, Michigan 94230
(313) 340-2957

KEYWORDS: Chef, manager, 4-star restaurant, fine dining, French cuisine, hire/fire, budgeting, organizing, plan menus, develop clientele, scheduling, parties, hands-on, energetic, courteous, fine wine/liquor, take-charge, cleanliness, dynamic, flexible, creative, Microsoft Word, Lotus 1-2-3, Windows.

SKILLS
- Creative, expressive individual
- Hands-on, team-oriented manager
- Personable with excellent communication skills
- Competent and flexible organizational skills
- Knowledgeable in all areas of French cuisine
- Microsoft Word, Lotus 1-2-2, and Windows computer skills

EMPLOYMENT HISTORY
Chef, **Le Blanc Chateau,** 1992–Present
- Created unique and exceptional menu offering all types of French cuisine
- Developed extensive wine collection
- Reviewed by local paper with a 4-star rating
- Increased business by 25%
- Maintained inventory and communicated with wholesalers
- Managed staff of five assistant chefs

Manager and Assistant Chef, **The Pine Log Inn,** 1985–1992
- Oversaw staff of 35 employees, ranging from maitre d' to support staff
- Increased business by 40%
- Hired, trained, and fired staff as necessary

Cook, **Martha's Grille,** 1980–1985
- Prepared varied menu for a busy 24-hour restaurant
- Ordered supplies and maintained inventory
- Arranged for parties and special occasions

EDUCATION:
Le Francais Alliance, Master Chef, 1992
Bachelor of Arts, Michigan State, Business, 1980

PROFESSIONAL ORGANIZATIONS:
National Association of Restaurant Managers
The French Alliance Association

Sample Electronic Resume

CHAPTER | 5

Writing a resume can be hard work. Make it easy on yourself. This chapter tells you how to make the process simpler and quicker. Not only will you save time and effort; you'll also wind up with a polished, professional-looking resume.

ROLL UP YOUR SLEEVES

INFORMATION YOU NEED BEFORE WRITING YOUR RESUME

A resume is not an autobiographical history of your entire life. You must be discriminating about what will go in and what will be left out. Whether you had full-time, part-time, or volunteer employment, the decision rests with the question, "Will it help you get the job you want?"

But first, you must collect all information that will have a bearing on your next job. Only then can you look back and decide what should be included.

THINGS YOU WILL NEED BEFORE YOU START

Don't sit down until you have within your reach:

1. Two sharpened pencils with erasers
2. A pencil sharpener
3. An 8 1/2" x 11" lined pad
4. A dictionary and a thesaurus
5. Any diplomas, certificates, or awards you received
6. Your employment history (dates, names of companies, job titles)
7. A cup of coffee, tea, water, or whatever stimulates your thinking
8. Peace and quiet

COLLECTING INFORMATION

The worksheets on the following pages will help you in gathering your work experience, educational history, and personal background into one comprehensive document. This document will serve as the database for your resume. Make as many copies of these worksheets as you think you'll need before filling any of them out.

Work Experience

Most job seekers include only their last three to four jobs in a resume, or they only go as far back as ten years. However, completing the information for each job experience you've had will help you during interviews. Having a good handle on your employment, the skills and knowledge you gained, your reasons for leaving, and the positive aspects of each job will prepare you for any question the interviewer might ask.

For each *and every* job you've had, supply the information requested:

Name of Employer: _____

Starting Date: _____

Salary: _____

Termination Date: _____

Type of Company: _____

City and State: _____

Job Title: _____

Duties You Performed: _____

_____

_____

Skills You Used: _____

_____

_____

Greatest Accomplishment: _____

_____

What You Liked Most: _____

_____

What You Liked Least: _____

_____

Reason for Leaving: _____

References: _____

_____

Educational Background

Provide the following information for *each* school and/or training program you attended:

Name of School or Training Program: _____

City and State: _____

Dates Attended: _____

Certificate or Diploma Received: _____

Major and/or Minor: _____

Grade Point Average: _____

Special Awards, Distinctions or Scholarships: _____

_____

_____

Internships: _____

_____

Entry Requirements: _____

_____

Special Courses Taken: _____

_____

Reasons for not Graduating or Completing Program:

_____

_____

Outside Activities, Clubs, Sports: _____

_____

_____

Special Skills

Expand upon the following skills, as they apply to you:

Foreign Language(s):

    Fluent in Reading: _____

    Fluent in Writing: _____

    Fluent in Speaking: _____

Computer Skills:

    Basic Knowledge: _____

    Hardware: _____

    Software: _____

    _____

Office Skills:

    Typing: _____

    Stenography: _____

    Office Equipment: _____

Technical (such as auto mechanics, construction, plumbing, etc.):

    _____

    _____

    _____

Communication:

    Written: _____

    _____

    Oral: _____

    _____

    Interpersonal: _____

    _____

Military Experience, Volunteer Experience, and Interests
Military History:

Branch of Service: _____

Rank: _____

Dates: _____

Special Skills or Training: _____

_____

Volunteer Experience:

Describe any volunteer job or community involvement you have partici-
pated in. It's not important to talk just about your paid experience. *All*
experience is valuable.

Name of Organization: _____

Your Title or Role: _____

Dates: _____

Type of Organization: _____

Skills or Work Performed: _____

_____

What You Received or Learned from the Experience: _____

_____

_____

Interests:

List those interests and hobbies that could be a good match for the job
you are seeking. For example, a home health aide who enjoys cooking
and baking would be a great asset in the field.

_____

_____

_____

_____

IN SHORT

In this chapter you explored the following topics for your resume:
- Work experience
- Educational background
- Special skills
- Military experience
- Volunteer experience
- Interests

The hard part is over. You are now ready to write your resume. Chapter 6 will assist you in customizing all the information you gathered into a personalized, unique document that will be geared to the job you are seeking.

CHAPTER | 6

In this chapter you'll actually write a chronological resume—one that is correct and concise, and showcases your skills and experience. And once you complete this chapter, you will be able to take it straight to the typist or go to your own computer for keyboarding and printing.

YOUR LIFE ON ONE PAGE

HOW TO WRITE YOUR RESUME

The information you include in your own resume will depend upon your educational background and your job experience. If you have held several jobs, internships, or volunteer positions, chances are that you have ample information for a strong resume. But if you have little work experience, you may want to develop one or more of the optional sections, such as volunteer work or interests.

At the end of this chapter is a blank form for a chronological resume. Once you've read and thought about all the parts of the resume, you can fill in that blank form. You may want to make several photocopies before you start, in case you change your mind about something.

IDENTIFICATION

Include your name (no nicknames, please), full address, and telephone number. Be sure to include your area code and zip code.

OBJECTIVE

Your real objective is probably to get a job that you will absolutely love. You would like to work in a fabulous firm with great possibilities for advancement, one with big bonuses, long vacations, and a great salary. Although this may be true, you, of course, won't be able to say it this way in your resume!

Your goal here is to develop a job objective that allows you flexibility and is not so narrow that it eliminates you from consideration for many opportunities. It should not be geared to a particular job, but to your area of interest within a particular industry. You will be more specific as you customize the cover letter that accompanies your resume.

In the objective, you should:

- Specify your target industry
- Never put a specific job title in your objective, unless you have a particular degree or certification, e.g., registered nurse, dental hygienist, optometrist
- Make your statement broad enough to cover more than one type of work or position. For example, John just completed his Associate's degree in marketing. Although he hopes to work in men's clothing sales in a department store setting, he has developed an objective that is more general. The objective he developed for his resume reads:

> To obtain a challenging position in marketing, in a retail or department store setting, where I can utilize my education and experience.

Think about the kind of job you want and the industry you are targeting. Write your own objective here. Later in the chapter you will transfer this objective onto your resume worksheet.

Objective:

_____

_____

_____

EXPERIENCE

List your work experience in reverse chronological order. Include only three to four jobs and don't go back farther than ten years. If you are currently employed, list your present job first. You now need to learn how to translate the description of what you do at work into resume talk, or the language of the resume. Each description of a job task should begin with an action verb that says what you did.

CASE STUDY—A CURRENT JOB

Marissa, a high school senior, has worked as a nurse aide since her junior year. She is writing her resume and describing her _current_ job. She thinks of five things she does at work: She gives patients baths, helps feed them, takes them for walks, writes down in the charts what they eat and what she does with them. She always talks to the patients because it seems to calm them down. She is also helpful to the nurses when they ask for assistance.

Translation:
- <u>assists</u> patients in ADL (activities of daily living)
- <u>ambulates</u> patients under supervision
- <u>records</u> progress notes clearly and accurately
- <u>reduces</u> patient anxiety by explaining all procedures

CASE STUDY—A FORMER JOB

John Kenyon was developing his resume for a job he had last summer in Home Mart. Although the salary was enough to pay for the insurance on his old Toyota, he was now a graduate and looking for full-time employment. At Home Mart, John had operated the cash register, counted money, handed in receipts, made minor repairs on office machines, restocked the shelves, and cleaned up after the store closed.

Translation:
- <u>operated</u> register and reconciled monies collected
- <u>conducted</u> inventory and restocked shelves
- <u>made</u> minor repairs to registers and office equipment
- <u>mopped, stripped,</u> and <u>waxed</u> floors, maintaining general appearance and cleanliness of store

The verbs have been underlined to draw your attention to them. Action verbs show you are *active*; you were doing something. For your present job, use present tense (*work, works*); for your past job(s), use past tense (*worked*).

On the next page is a list you can use to develop your own job task descriptions. Use it to jog your memory about the kinds of work you've done and to see which words to use to describe that work.

CINDY'S WORK EXPERIENCE

Read the following scenario. Then develop four statements that Cindy could use on her resume:

> Cindy Jamison opened the swimming pool at the Y every Tuesday, Thursday, and Saturday. After scheduling swim times for various youth groups and senior citizen groups, she organized swim meets and publicized the competitions. She trained and provided orientation for new lifeguards.

_____

_____

_____

_____

Possible Answers:
- <u>established</u> pool schedules for junior and senior swimmers
- <u>organized</u> interagency swim meets
- <u>created</u> marketing materials and publicized events
- <u>provided</u> staff training for new lifeguards

RESUME ACTION WORDS

accelerated	accessed	accomplished
accounted for	accumulated	acquired
adapted	administered	advertised
advised	analyzed	assisted
assured	began	budgeted
calculated	changed	collated
charted	collected	completed
composed	computed	coordinated
created	concluded	conserved
consolidated	contributed	corrected
counseled	developed	designed
debugged	directed	disseminated
distributed	earned	edited
established	emphasized	employed
engineered	evaluated	expanded
facilitated	finished	formulated
granted	guaranteed	guided
headed	helped	hired
identified	included	increased
illustrated	initiated	installed
maintained	managed	marketed
mastered	maximized	modernized
modified	motivated	negotiated
notified	obtained	opened
operated	ordered	originated
participated	performed	persuaded
pinpointed	planned	prepared
presented	projected	promoted
proved	publicized	purchased
realized	recommended	reduced
received	reconciled	reconstructed
recorded	recruited	reduced
reinforced	replaced	reported
requested	restored	retrained
revised	saved	scheduled
screened	secured	selected
served	started	streamlined
strengthened	submitted	supported
systematized	taught	tested
trained	transferred	translated
updated	upgraded	used
utilized	validated	verified
won	worked	wrote

YOUR OWN WORK EXPERIENCE

Think about one of the jobs you have held. List five things that your did at that job.

_____

_____

_____

_____

_____

Write down one thing that you were most proud of at your last job. This may help you embellish your task descriptions.

_____

_____

Now look at the verbs in the list, Resume Action Words. Translate those tasks into resume language.

_____

_____

_____

_____

_____

Look the list over. Make sure that the most important task comes first. Number from the most important to least important now.

EDUCATION

Include all information about your academic background. In reverse chronological order, list college attended, training or technical school, high school or GED program, month and year you graduated, major, and courses related to objective. Mention positive aspects of your academic career, such as Dean's List and honors. If you did not complete a degree, list the number of credits you attained. If you are currently enrolled in school, you may want to place the education section directly under your objective.

SKILLS

List any specific skills that you have not included earlier in your resume. For example, computer hardware and software expertise, equipment you can operate, foreign languages spoken, typing at 50wpm, license to drive a truck, certified in CPR, are all important skills to cite, if you have them.

OPTIONAL SECTIONS

If you have had little work experience, your one-page resume may look a little sparse. However, you may have had other experiences that have given you work-related skills you can write about.

VOLUNTEER WORK

You can use this section to discuss your volunteer work or involvement in a professional association. Perhaps you drive for your town's volunteer rescue unit, lead an Eagle Scout Troop, or work in the local hospital. Each of these experiences provides you with skills that may be relevant to your job search. As a volunteer rescuer, you probably:

Respond to crisis situations in a professional manner.
Provide appropriate emergency medical interventions.

If you have volunteer experience, develop your task descriptions in the same manner you would for paid employment.

INTERESTS

If you have any unusual interests, you can list them here. These may catch the eye of an employer and may become a topic for conversation during your interview. Avoid talking about interests that many people have, like reading or sewing. Don't invent an unusual interest; however, if you enjoy sky diving, wilderness exploration, or are a frequent exhibitor in art shows, for example, mention it in this section.

REFERENCES

You must ask people to give you references. These may be professors, teachers, employers, professional acquaintances, or personal friends who can talk about the strength of your character, your talents, and your particular skills. References will have work to do if you are being considered for a job. They may have to speak to potential employers on the phone or to write letters on your behalf. These may be time-consuming activities; make sure that your references are willing to take that time.

Asking your current boss to give you a reference is a sensitive issue. If you have a good relationship with her and have told her that you are job hunting, go ahead. If you are keeping your job-searching activities a secret, better ask someone else.

Be sure that you choose your references wisely. Never list a reference if you haven't asked them if they are willing to be your reference. At the bottom of your resume, make the statement: "References available upon request."

WRITE YOUR DRAFT

Use the worksheet at the end of this chapter to develop your resume on paper. Make some copies before you start, and use a pencil so that it will be easy to make changes as you review your work.

RESUME TIPS

Remember, as you sit down to write your resume:

- Use action verbs
- Emphasize your achievements
- Provide numbers and statistics to dramatize your point
- Promote yourself
- Always tell the truth
- Emphasize by **bolding,** CAPITALIZING, and underlining

Finally, proofread all written materials. Even if you have worked with a professional typist, it is your resume and you are responsible for checking that it is correct. After all, you are the one who will be sending it out!

Then, as you put the final touches on that resume and get it ready to mail:
- Make sure it fits all on one page
- Use standard letter size paper
- Cream or white are acceptable paper colors
- Make high-quality copies that are easy to read
- Be sure that your cover letters match

IN SHORT

Congratulations, you have completed your resume. In it you've:
- Created a targeted but flexible objective
- Listed your work experience in reverse order, using action verbs
- Listed your education, again in reverse order
- Described other work-related skills
- Mentioned volunteer work and/or interests to supplement your work experience
- Concluded with "references available on request" (and have three people willing to give you good references)

You're now ready to begin your search!

RESUME

Name_____

Address_____

Phone (area code) _____

OBJECTIVE: _____

_____

_____

EXPERIENCE: _____

Name of Company (most recent)   City, State

_____ _____

Date   Job Title

- _____

_____

- _____

_____

- _____

_____

- _____

_____

Name of Company (most recent)   City, State

Date   Job Title

- _____

  _____

- _____

  _____

- _____

  _____

- _____

  _____

EDUCATION:

Date   School   City, State

Degree, Diploma, Certificate, or credits attained

Date   School   City, State

Degree, Diploma, Certificate, or credits attained

Date   School   City, State

Degree, Diploma, Certificate, or credits attained

SKILLS: *List any specialized skills that you did not list in the body of your resume.*

_____

_____

_____

SPECIAL CERTIFICATES AWARDS, or COMMUNITY SERVICE:

_____

_____

_____

INTERESTS: _____

(Optional) _____

_____

REFERENCES: Furnished upon request

CHAPTER | 7

A cover letter is an important job hunting tool; it accompanies your resume whenever you apply for a position. This chapter explains how to write effective cover letters that make you look and sound like the terrific job candidate you are.

THE RESUME'S COMPANION
COVER LETTERS

When Danny and Sandy belt out, "We go together," in the finale of the movie *Grease*, they could have been singing about cover letters and resumes. They do go together, and a good cover letter will get the reader to turn the page to your resume.

WHY YOU NEED A GOOD COVER LETTER

It's virtually impossible to modify your resume for each and every potential job. This is why you need cover letters; they provide you with the opportunity to customize your correspondence to meet the particulars of a specific job. Cover letters:

- Accompany *every* single resume you send out
- Are concise and geared to the position you are seeking
- Are one page long and usually contain three (but no more than four) paragraphs
- Clearly and specifically state why you are applying for the position
- Are written only to the person responsible for hiring and only for the position open (using one standard form letter for every job you apply for will only serve to keep you out of the running because employers will know the difference)

TRUE STORY

Avoid Cover Letter Bloopers

Department head Ann Sommers was screening resume packets that had come into her office in response to an ad. She expected that it would take quite a while to read the cover letters in the stack of twenty. She planned to select a few candidates who would be invited for an interview. Her job took a much shorter time than she expected because she was able to eliminate people without even looking at their resumes. Their cover letters made a bad impression:

#1 was written on a page torn from a notebook
#2 was a standard form letter
#3 was written in pencil
#4 had grammatical errors in it
#5 was addressed, "Dear Ann"
#6 said nothing about the advertised position
#7 had three misspelled words in it
#8 was written on a flowery note card
#9 was illegible and had a coffee stain on the bottom
#10 had seven typographical errors in it

Poorly presented cover letters like the ones Ann Sommers had to read guarantee that the reader will not bother to turn the page and give serious consideration to the accompanying resume. Cover letters must be correct in every way and look appealing. They should be typed in correct form and sent on good-quality stationery that matches your resume.

COVER LETTER FORMAT

The format for a cover letter is standard, and your letters should conform to acceptable business practice. All cover letters have six basic elements, as you'll see in the two sample cover letters at the end of this chapter. The block format of the first is cleaner and more modern, but also a bit more rigid; the second's indented paragraphs is a more classic style. Choose which of the two you like best and use its format as a model for your own.

THE HEADING

Begin your heading about 1 inch below the top of your page. No matter what style business letter you select, the heading always includes:

Your address
City, State, Zip Code
Date

THE INSIDE ADDRESS

The inside address specifies the name and title of the person to whom you are writing and the full address of the company. It's essential that you write to a *person*, not to a department. Letters are read by people. Putting the name of the person who has the power to hire you on the letter will give you a better chance that he or she will read it.

Don't send off a letter when you're lacking full information for the inside address. But what, then, do you do if for instance you do not know the name of the director of personnel or the manager of the department? Get on the telephone. It only takes one or two calls to the company to find the name of the person who will be interviewing.

Practice

Look at this help-wanted advertisement for an entry-level job:

> Import company seeks recent grad who is a quick learner to make two all expense annual trips to China to assist buyer of electric bicycles, toys, and novelties. Must be mature, a team player and willing to travel. Knowledge of Chinese desirable. Fax resume and cover letter to: General Imports Inc., fax # (796) 873-8600.

In order to develop the inside address, you will need to do one of the following:

a. Call the newspaper and ask for the telephone number of the company who placed the ad

b. Fax your cover letter and resume to General Imports Inc., To Whom It May Concern

c. Call information in that area code (796) and ask the operator for the number of the General Imports Inc. Then call the company and ask for name of the personnel director.

Answer: c. The most efficient method for accessing the name and title you need to respond to the advertisement is making a phone call directly to the company. What if an ad uses a Post Office Box number? You can call the Postmaster General in your city. Most post offices will provide you with the name and location of the company.

THE SALUTATION

The most appropriate greeting in a cover letter is:

Dear Dr. Evans:
or
Dear Ms. Williams:

Sometimes agencies and companies eliminate the possibility for calls by listing a box number, c/o (care of) the newspaper. If you run into a situation like this, use Dear Personnel Director: or Dear Chair, Search Committee. The salutation is always followed by a colon (:).

THE BODY

The body of your cover letter should contain, usually, three paragraphs.

Paragraph One

The first paragraph of the letter itself establishes:

- Why you are writing
- What position you are applying for
- How you found out about the position

Here's an example of a first paragraph of a cover letter sent in response to an ad:

Dear Ms. Rettle:

I am writing in response to the teaching position available in your school district advertised in the *Florida Sun Times* on Sunday, April 20, 1997.

And this is an example of a cover letter in response to a networking connection:

Dear Mr. Cutler:

I am writing at the recommendation of Mr. Jack Rafferty, your company's comptroller. Mr. Rafferty felt that my expertise in computer programming would make a good match for the programmer position now open in your firm.

Paragraph Two

The second paragraph provides you with the opportunity to match your unique skills and abilities with those required for the position. You need to direct the employer to your resume and then state those assets that do not appear on your resume but that qualify you for that position.

Think about yourself, your values, attitudes, and experience. What *doesn't* your resume state about you that may interest a potential employer? Think about your transferable skills and those important life experiences that state that you are a well-rounded, community-minded, articulate, flexible, hard-working individual with excellent communication skills. (If necessary, review Chapter 1, where you identified your special skills and talents.)

In paragraph two you might also mention your volunteer work, specialized training, fundraising experience, or, why, for example, there is an employment gap on your resume.

Here's an example of a cover letter's the second paragraph:

> As you can see from my resume, I have spent the last twelve years in Chicago's Board of Education for Special Students. I was instrumental in developing the district's award-winning science curriculum, as well as the Science Student of the Year competition. Teaching science to children of special needs is a challenge I find exciting and extremely rewarding.

If you are writing in response to an ad, key words within the ad signal characteristics that are important to the employer. Paragraph two of your cover letter can incorporate these keywords to tailor your skills to the job advertised.

Practice

Look at the following classified ad. List the key words that the employer has signaled as important:

> Admissions Coordinator
> Midtown Prep School seeking energetic, detail-oriented, communicator w/exc. phone skills for admissions and recruitment work. Must be committed to working with young people. Strong people skills and ability to work with team a must. Mail cover letter and resume to S. Kramer, ABD Academy, 329 Stratford Ave., NW, Washington, D.C.

List five key words or phrases that you would use in a cover letter to this company:

_____

_____

_____

_____

_____

Answer: Any five of the following could be included: energetic, detail-oriented, good communicator, excellent phone skills, committed, strong people skills, team player.

Paragraph Three

The third paragraph is your closing paragraph. It states your appreciation for the employer's time and consideration, and when you will contact him or her to set up an appointment. For example:

> I want to thank you for your consideration of my resume. I will be calling on Monday, March 23, to see if we can set up a convenient time to meet. I look forward to speaking with you next week.

You absolutely, positively must follow up on all correspondence. As hard as it might be, it is crucial that you follow up on each and every cover letter you send. If you say you are going to call on a particular day, make the call!

Helpful Hint: Prepare a short script for calling. Practice in front of a mirror, or even better, use a tape recorder to see how you sound. Say it and do it.

The Closing

An acceptable closing is Yours truly, or Very truly yours, or Sincerely. Only the first word in the closing is capitalized. The correct punctuation after the closing is always a comma (,).

Don't forget to sign your letter. You should place your signature between the closing and your full typed name. A signature is always written within the allotted space. Even if your handwriting is normally sloppy and hard to read, your signature on cover letters should be legible and neat, and it should stay within the margins. And happy faces and other unique ways in which you dot your i's or cross your t's have no place in business correspondence! Use black or blue ink.

COVER LETTER TIPS

Some final tips on preparing your cover letter:

- Presentation, accuracy, correctness, and effectiveness of expression reveal a great deal about the pride you take in your work.
- Watch out for spelling demons, repetitious language, incorrect usage, and grammar traps.
- Have on hand a supply of stationery, a dictionary, thesaurus, and a basic grammar book, such as the LearningExpress book *Writing Skills in 20 Minutes a Day.*
- Proofread, proofread, proofread. The spell check tool on your computer does not take the place of careful editing and proofreading. Computers cannot tell whether *to, too,* or *two* is correct in your context.
- Before mailing anything, ask someone else to read your letter.

IN SHORT

A cover letter is an important opportunity to give potential employers information that is not specifically stated in your resume:

- Paragraph One states what job you're applying for and how you found out about it.
- Paragraph Two matches your skills and experience with those required for the job available.
- Paragraph Three closes the letter with a thank you and a promise to follow up with a phone call.

Well written, concise, and interesting letters will pique the interest of the reader and get you to the next stage of your job search—the interview.

498 Blackstone Drive
Malvern, New York 13341

February 15, 1997

Mr. Jack Sample
Managing Director
All City Clubs, Inc.
213 West 33 Street, Suite 403
New York, NY 11093

Dear Mr. Sample:

Enclosed is my resume in application for the Counselor Training Program that was advertised in the *New York Times* on Saturday, February 15, 1997.

I am a recent high school graduate with strong communication skills and a firm commitment to working with young people. As an Eagle Scout and honor student, I have always been active in community organizations. My time as a volunteer in the YMCA tutoring program was well spent, and the personal rewards gained from working with young people influenced and shaped my career goals. I feel confident that I would make an excellent candidate for your counselor training program.

I want to thank you for your time and consideration. I will call on Wednesday, February 21, to discuss a convenient time to meet. I look forward to speaking with you.

Yours truly,

David Bartlett

Enc.

Cover Letter Sample A

4839 Elvin Avenue
Preston, Alabama 40303
February 3, 1997

Ms. Charline Hynes
Director of Personnel
Middlesex County Hospital
329 Broadway
Preston, Alabama 40303

Dear Ms. Hynes:

I am writing concerning the article in Saturday's *Evening Post* regarding the expansion of the nurse's aide department at Middlesex County Hospital. As a recently graduated certified nurse's aide, I am very interested in exploring career opportunities within your hospital.

As you can see from the enclosed my resume, I have recently completed a course in nurse's aide training and phlebotomy. In order to meet national licensing requirements, I have completed over 120 venipunctures and 75 finger sticks. During this training, I worked with patients of all ages, including infants on the neonatal floor. I certainly believe in lifelong education and will continue to broaden my clinical abilities when opportunities arise.

I would be pleased to meet you to discuss opportunities at Middlesex, and I will call next Tuesday, February 9, to see when you are available to meet. Thank you for your time and consideration. I look forward to meeting you soon.

Sincerely yours,

Jacqueline Baynes

Enc.

Cover Letter Sample B

CHAPTER | 8

In this chapter you will preview many job-hunting techniques, learn which are most effective, and begin to map out your game plan. With this information in hand, you can go on to the chapters that cover specific job-seeking strategies.

THE SEARCH IS ON
AN OVERVIEW OF JOB-SEEKING METHODS

I n baseball, the quickest way to reach home plate is to hit a home run. But you can also score runs by hitting ground rule doubles, bunts, and singles. So, too, in the job search game: You can score big time right away—if you're lucky and in the right place, at the right time—or, like most people, you can get to home plate by taking one base (step) at a time.

There are jobs out there and you need to find the one that's right for you. You'll always have competition when you're job seeking because there will always be other people looking for jobs at the same time as you. But remember that there are always new jobs opening up all the time, every day. Employees leave firms when they:

- Take buy outs and retire
- Make career transitions
- Relocate
- Take leaves of absence or become disabled

In addition, new jobs are always being created in response to the need for new products, new technologies, and new services. You may be *job* seeking, but employers are *employee* seeking at the same time.

The best way to find the right job is to use a combination of job-search techniques that will get you interviews. Then you will be able to sell yourself in person.

STRATEGIES TO GET INTERVIEWS

There are multiple ways to gather information and to learn about industries and available jobs. You can:

- Network with friends, family, and colleagues
- Conduct research and contact companies directly
- Answer classified ads in newspapers, professional journals, and trade papers
- Attend job fairs and open houses
- Go on-line and search company home pages and job centers
- Contact the placement office of your school
- Work with support groups
- Canvas community and civic associations
- Use an employment agency
- Look in the Yellow Pages and "cold call"
- Check state employment service centers
- Call employment hot lines in specific companies

THE MOST EFFECTIVE STRATEGIES

Career development specialists have found through experience that *directly contacting targeted companies* and *networking* are the job-search methods that give the best results. The overwhelming majority of jobs— 85 to 90 percent of them—are found these ways. They work because they lead to jobs that are often not advertised widely, jobs that few people may know about—the hidden job market, so to speak.

There's nothing difficult or special about networking. You simply start telling people you know—anybody and everybody—that you're looking for a job in such and such areas, doing whatever it is you want to do. Most people won't be able to help you directly, but some may know of a job opening, or know of someone who works in that field, or perhaps they'll know someone who knows someone. And so it goes.

Applying directly to companies means doing some research to find out which companies are hiring now or may be in the future, to find out who you might write to or call for interviews for jobs that have never been posted or advertised.

These methods are so effective that two entire chapters—chapters 9 and 10—are devoted to telling you exactly how to use them. They're the focus of effective job searches. Most of your time and energy, three out of five days in your "work week," should be devoted to networking and direct contact. In baseball lingo, using networking and direct contact will give you a batting average between 600 and 700.

OTHER STRATEGIES

There are other techniques that can—and should—be used along with networking and direct contact (see Chapters 11 and 12). Although the odds of getting a job with these strategies are lower, they shouldn't be ignored; people do find jobs these ways. To keep on track, plan to use no more than two of these other methods at a time, and assign two days a week (or one-fourth of your time) for them.

ESTABLISHING A ROUTINE

Once you have decided on your strategies, establish a schedule and then stick to it. Even if you were employed, you would not be working seven days a week, 24 hours a day. Plan a regular 35-hour work week for job hunting. Promise yourself a special reward if you stick to your schedule—and then give yourself that treat!

LOOKING FOR WORK PART-TIME

If you are conducting your job search while working part time, you'll be juggling several different activities at the same time and will need to be super organized.

Look at your work schedule. Block out the times when you're not working. Once you have identified the hours available for job hunting, you will need to develop a schedule for the library, for making phone calls, and for developing your written materials.

And since you are working, not sitting home waiting for return calls, you will need to purchase an answering machine. Perhaps you will want to invest in a beeper, one that gives you the caller's name and phone number. You can then respond to calls before work, during your lunch hour, or at the end of your work day.

IN SHORT

Networking and targeted direct contact are the central focus of an effective job search. In the next chapters you will learn more about these and other search methods. But don't use more than four different strategies at any one time. Your game plan will look like this (fill in the other two methods of your choice):

1. Networking

2 Direct contact

3 _____

4. _____

Remember:

- Looking for work is your job now.
- Set up a schedule and stick to it.
- Give yourself a treat—you've gotten this far, you deserve it!

CHAPTER | 9

Now that you've identified
your target job market,
your skills, and those
qualities that make you
an asset to an employer,
you know what you are
selling. This chapter will
teach you how to network:
how to meet potential
employers who are hiring
people to do the work
you want to do.

OPEN SESAME
THE MAGIC OF NETWORKING

Looking for a job is hard work. There are the obvious places to look, like newspaper ads. And then there is the "hidden job market," those positions that aren't advertised in papers for all the world (and your competition) to see. In fairy tales, "Open Sesame" and "Abracadabra" yield magic. In the real world of work, the magic word for getting access to that hidden job market is networking. In fact, someone you meet today may be the link to your very next job!

TRUE STORY

Casting a Wide Net Pays Off

When Joe was laid off from his job as a fiscal manager of an HMO, his first impulse was to keep it a secret. However, the realities of rent and family pressured him to take action. On the day after "layoff day" Joe revised his resume and brought it up to date.

Next, he sat down at his computer and he wrote a basic cover letter that could easily be modified. He began to tell people about his situation. By the end of week one he had:

- Arranged an informational meeting with a contact from his previous job
- Spoken with the boss of his college roommate's brother
- Met with the CEO of an expanding medical software company
- Called six referrals given to him by his mother-in-law
- Spoken to the finance director of the agency where his wife worked
- Faxed seventeen copies of his resume to employer contacts recommended by college friends
- Kept a dated record of all his contacts

He told everyone he met or spoke with that he was looking for a position in health care management or technology.

In a short time, Joe had created a personal network that had expanded exponentially. Four weeks later, he accepted a position.

CONTACTS COME NATURALLY

Have you ever met someone at a party and after a brief conversation discovered that you have a mutual friend? Or that you grew up just several blocks from one another in a town hundreds of miles away? Experiences like this remind you that it really *is* a small world.

In any job search, you use networking to make connections to people you don't already know. These connections will result in information and interviews that may lead to a job. You probably haven't thought about it, but you use networking quite naturally in many different contexts of your life already.

When you want to buy a car, you call around to see if any of your friends know someone who has the car you are thinking about. That's networking. When you want to choose a college, you speak to many people, some of whom have been referred to you by others. That's networking. And when you plan a vacation, you call for brochures, decide where you want to go, ask your friends if they know anyone who has been there, and then shop for the best deal. You're a networker.

Networking in a job search requires the same skills and organizational strategies that you've already used. In order to be an effective networker in a job search you need to be sure of:

What you are selling—you
    and
Who the buyers should be—your job target

Networking is the method through which you will find out the names of the buyers (in other words, possible employers) so that you can tell them about yourself.

GETTING READY TO NETWORK

Networking is a process that has organized steps and an overall strategic plan. In order to be an effective networker, you need to have information at your fingertips.

STEP 1: THINK ABOUT YOURSELF

Think of your own skills in terms of positive workplace language. Desirable workers are those with:

- Strong basic skills
- Creative thinking and problem-solving skills
- Positive personal qualities such as self-management, flexibility, responsibility, tact, integrity, and the ability to work as part of a team

STEP 2: SUMMARIZE YOUR CAREER GOALS

You have already identified your match in Chapter 2. Summarize your personal career goals here. Fill in the following chart.

I am looking for work in the field of

_____

I am well suited to this work because (skills, interests, experience)

_____

_____

My best qualities and skills are

_____

_____

The work environment I am most interested is (large/small company, for profit/not for profit)

_____

The vocabulary of work is important. What have you learned from academic study and training? List two school-related skills that are relevant to your job target, for example, "knowledge of management principles" or "solid foundation in biochemistry."

_____

_____

STEP 3: COPY RESUMES

Prepare fifty copies of your resume on quality paper. Be sure have a large enough supply of paper to print cover letters and thank-you notes that match.

STEP 4: CREATE A RECORD FILE FOR CONTACTS

Buy 4 x 6 inch index cards and create a format for keeping track of your contacts, their referrals, your action and the date, and all follow-up activity.

Each new lead and follow-up must be charted. Look at the sample cards at the end of this chapter. They're designed for notes that you can then transfer into the Job Seeking Strategy Planning Record in chapter 11. You may wish to copy this record form so that you can fill it in and keep it separate from the book. After all, you want to make sure that you remember who led you to whom!

STEP 5: DEVELOP YOUR CONTACT LIST
Make a list of all the people you know. Remember, they may not be in a position to offer you a job, but they may have just the referral you are looking for. Your list might include:
- Family members
- Friends
- Neighbors
- School associates
- Fellow job seekers
- Friends from your gym or sports team
- Former teachers
- Colleagues from your last job or the job before that
- The references on your resume
- People from community groups you belong to
- Members of your place of worship

These are the people who will may very well lead you to other people you don't know yet who may be able to help you locate a job.

STEP 6: PREPARE YOUR PHONE SCRIPTS
Develop your scripts for calling. Using the information you have just summarized, your resume, and workplace vocabulary, develop your scripts. In just 90 seconds you should be able to establish who you are and why you are calling. If you have been given a contact to get general information, you can say that you have no reason to believe that a position is available right now but you would like an opportunity to explore the market. Be appreciative of the person's valuable time. You might say:

Hello. I'm calling at the suggestion of John Henry, who plays on my softball team. John mentioned that you work in an HMO and since he knows that I am completing a certificate program in medical management, he thought that you would be a good person to speak with about the field. Would you be able to spare about 20 minutes to meet with me at your convenience and share your expertise? Could you suggest someone else I might speak with? I really appreciate your time and insights.

If a networking contact has gotten you the name of a potential employer, your script might sound a little different:

Hello, I'm calling at the suggestion of Mr. John Henry who is familiar with my training and experience in the fiscal area of health care management. John mentioned that he heard that you had an opening in your firm and felt that I would be a good match for that position in terms of my skills, creativity, and management style. I would like to meet with you at your convenience to discuss the position. Would you prefer my resume beforehand or shall I bring it with me?

Creating Your Own Scripts

Think about some situations you might find yourself in the next few weeks and write a short script for each:

1. Develop a script for calling the friend of someone you met at a barbecue last week who works in your target job market.
2. Develop a script for calling a potential employer who was referred to you by a former teacher.
3. Choose someone from your own personal network list. Create your own script, one that you will use with your other contacts and referrals.

Practice

Practice your scripts often so that they sound natural. Ask a friend or relative to listen to you. Better still, call yourself and record the conversation on your answering machine. That will give you a chance to review the content of your message as well as your tone and presentation.

KEEP YOUR GOALS IN MIND

Networking requires that you use the tools you have just prepared in an organized, focused, and confident manner. Make your calls. Try to establish rapport and make a positive impression. You never know whom this person may know. Make notes of the call using your index cards. Try not to hang up without getting a meeting, an interview, or a referral first.

FOLLOW UP

Send a thank-you note to the person who has taken time to speak with you. Even if a conversation you had with an employer didn't seem to lead anywhere, still follow up and send a resume. That person may not have a job for you right now, but she has lots of colleagues who might be looking for a person with just your qualifications two weeks or so down the road.

When your networking has led you to an employer, don't forget to express your interest in the company and reiterate why you would be an asset. You may want to follow up with another call in several weeks. Try to collect good relationships, not just phone numbers and business cards.

TRUE STORY

A Simple "Thank You" Can Pay Off

Richard interviewed for a position with a publishing company. He established very good rapport with the interviewer; however, he did not get the position; another candidate was chosen for the job. Richard was disappointed, but he called his interviewer to thank him and to ask him to keep him in mind for future opportunities.

Two months after the interview, Richard got a call from this new contact who recommended him to a colleague for another publishing position that sounds very interesting. And guess what? Richard has been invited in for an interview.

OTHER OPPORTUNITIES FOR NETWORKING

A network can never get too large. Here are some other ways to broaden yours.

Job Search Support Groups

These groups of people who are in the job market can give you a personal boost, help you to stay focused, and provide very practical advice and information. Many put on how-to presentations, facilitate discussion groups, and share job hunting directories, books and other references. Support groups may charge a membership fee, so ask if there is a cost. You can learn about support groups by buying the *National Business Employment Weekly* or by calling the local office of the U.S. Department of Labor.

Professional Associations

Many professional associations have regional chapters that hold regular meetings, which are sometimes open to the public. Take advantage of them! They're great opportunities for you to network with people who work in your field or one related to it. Don't know where to begin? Go to the library and look in the *Encyclopedia of Associations*. It's an excellent directory of hundreds of organizations, many of which are professional associations. Each listing includes brief information about membership and provides a phone number that you can call to get more information about a chapter near you. Find out when it meets and make it your business to attend. Be ready to take notes and to make connections.

IN SHORT

You've used networking skills, probably many times already in your life. Perhaps you called around to ask whether a particular instructor was a "hard marker" or assigned a term paper. Maybe you asked friends for the name of a jeweler when looking for a special gift.

Networking may feel different when you are looking for a job, but it's really very much the same. Just follow these steps:

- List your career goals
- Make copies of your resume
- Create a simple system for keeping notes
- Begin a contact list by starting with people you know
- Prepare phone scripts and practice them
- Get on the phone and begin calling
- Send thank-you's
- Attend meetings of support group and professional organizations for advice and more contacts

LearningExpress

20 Academy Street, P.O. Box 7100, Norwalk, CT 06852-9879

To provide you with the best test prep, basic skills, and
career materials, we would appreciate your help.
Please answer the following questions and return this postage paid piece.
Thank you for your time!

Name : _____

Address : _____

_____

Age : _____ Sex : ☐ Male ☐ Female

Highest Level of School Completed : ☐ High School ☐ College

1) I am currently :

    A student — Year/level: _____

    Employed — Job title: _____

    Other — Please explain: _____

2) Jobs/careers of interest to me are :

    1. _____

    2. _____

    3. _____

3) If you are a student, did your guidance/career counselor provide
you with job information/materials? _____

4) What newspapers and/or magazines do you subscribe to or
read regularly? _____

_____

5) Do you own a computer? _____

    If so, do you have Internet access? _____

    How often do you go on-line? _____

6) The last time you visited a bookstore, did you make a purchase?

_____

Have you purchased career-related materials from bookstores?

_____

7) Do you subscribe to cable TV? _____

    Which channels to you watch regularly (please give network
    letters rather than channel numbers)?

_____

_____

8) Which radio stations do you listen to regularly (please give call
    letters and city name)?

_____

_____

9) How did you hear about the book you just purchased from
    LearningExpress?

    An ad? _____

    If so, where? _____

    An order form in the back of another book? _____

    A recommendation? _____

    A bookstore? _____

    Other? _____

10) Title of the book this card came from:

_____

LearningExpress books are also available in the test prep/study guide section of your local bookstore.

NO POSTAGE
NECESSARY
IF MAILED
IN THE
UNITED STATES

BUSINESS REPLY MAIL
FIRST CLASS MAIL   PERMIT NO. 150   NORWALK, CT

POSTAGE TO BE PAID BY THE ADDRESSEE

LearningExpress
20 Academy Street
P.O. Box 7100
Norwalk, CT 06852-9879

LEARNINGEXPRESS

The leading publisher of customized career and test preparation books!

LearningExpress is an affiliate of Random House, Inc.

Contact From:

Name	Company & Phone	Action
1.		
2.		
3.		

Referred me to:

Name	Agency & Phone	Action
1.		
2.		
3.		

Contact From: *Mother-in-law*   9/30

Name	Company & Phone	Action
1. Ruth Ogland	Seaford Hosp. 293-6000 ext. 900	Sent resume *
2.		
3.		* Make follow-up call

Referred me to:

Name	Agency & Phone	Action
1. Brian Jasper	Amherst Med. Cent. 299-1579	Left mess. *
2. Deane Wilson	Egmont Nursing Home 324 Manor Ave	Apt. 10/12, 10 a.m. Rm. 306 Main Bldg.
3. Dr. Kenig	Health Corp 396-4050	* Called for appt., left message

* Call back!

Sample Network Contact Card (4 x 6)

CHAPTER | 10

Where's the best place to look for the types of jobs you want? Obviously, in those companies that have such jobs. But how do you know which companies have which jobs? You do research. In this chapter you'll learn how to do this research.

CREATING OPPORTUNITIES
TARGETED DIRECT CONTACT

Targeted direct contact is extremely effective. But it requires research, good writing skills, and a confident, focused telephone manner. In Chapter 3 you identified your job target and the kinds of employers who hire people for this kind of work. Now it is time for targeting your search. You will:

- Decide what types of companies you want to research, based on your field
- Research the names of companies who hire people for the kind of work you do and to learn industry trends
- Compile a list of target companies
- Prioritize your choices

- Send out a resume and cover letter to each of these companies
- Follow up with a phone call
- Do more research once you are called for an interview

PHASE ONE: RESEARCH FOR CALLS AND LETTERS

You already know how to do research because you did it in school when you had papers to write or oral presentations to deliver. You identified your topic and went to the library, where you looked for references in books, articles, and journals. These familiar skills are the ones you will now use in your job search.

TRUE STORY

Focus on Your Priorities

When a young teacher moved to the suburbs, she did not want to have more than a 40-minute commute to work each morning. She wanted to work in an intermediate school and would accept employment in a public, private, or parochial institution. Geography was very important to her. She bought a map of her area and drew a circle with a radius of 30 miles.

She called the school districts that fell within her circle and identified all the schools. She researched the schools, customized her cover letters, and sent mailings to 76 of them. Within a week, she followed up with phone calls. She was invited to three interviews and accepted a teaching position in a school 23 minutes from her house.

WHY RESEARCH IS IMPORTANT

You want a potential employer to choose you from a large applicant pool. And she will if, in every way, you demonstrate that you have drive, ambition, energy, strong skills and personal assets—and knowledge about her company. Research will help you select your targets, customize your cover letters to include information you have learned about the company, speak knowledgeably in follow-up phone calls, and make a strong impression at an interview.

To help you keep good records and remind you of the information that you should have, take a look now at the sample Research Record form at the end of this chapter. It's a good idea to make several copies of this form so you can complete one for each target company.

THE LIBRARY—A GOLDMINE OF INFORMATION

Go to your library and speak with the librarian. Become familiar with the layout. In many libraries there are sections devoted entirely to job market information. In this first phase of research, you want to gather enough information to sound knowledgeable on the phone and in your cover letter so that you will be called for an interview.

Look for News and Trends

You are looking for company names and industry trends such as a new technology or major merger—topics that will give you a some information to mention when contacting employers.

Extensive information is not necessary in your first round of research. This is the time to *scan* the periodicals for recent articles about industries and companies and to make lists of potential places for employment. Take the extra time to take careful and complete notes. (Use the Research Record form at the end of this chapter for note taking.) You will add to this information later, when preparing for your interview.

Take Advantage of the Librarian's Expertise

Librarians are extremely well-trained information specialists. Explain to yours that you're looking for information about your target industry in general, and about specific companies and their finances, growth projections, professional associations, trade publications, key players, new products, and emerging trends.

USEFUL DIRECTORIES OF ALL SORTS

A good place to begin your research is *Directories In Print*, by Gale Research. This volume contains over 15,000 listings of directories indexed by key words. In it you will find general directories, and directories of professional associations, of trade publications, of financial publications, of international corporations, and of corporate personnel.

General Directories

General directories may point the way to more industry-specific resources. As a starting point you can use:

Guide to American Directories. Information on 5,000 directories in all professional and mercantile categories

Standard and Poor's Registry of Corporations, Directors, and Executives. Over 26,000 American and Canadian firms included, with information about officers, employees, industry, and products.

There are also directories of foreign-owned companies that operate in the United States.

Specialized Directories

Industries have their own specialized directories. Check with your librarian about sources for particular industries. A valuable source of information that includes most industries, their associations, and trade publications can be found in the *JobBank* series, an excellent resource for job seekers. These books are available in local book stores at a reasonable price and together they target 30 different geographic areas of the United States. Each volume contains an enormous amount of information, such as employers (large and small), industry associations, and industry-specific publications.

Let's say that you have majored in chemistry and are interested in pharmaceutical sales in Connecticut. The *JobBank* will provide a list of all the pharmaceutical companies within the region, their addresses, corporate contacts, and company information. You will also find a listing of contacts for specific industry publications and associations.

Specific Company Information

Here are some good general business directories:

Dun and Bradstreet Million Dollar Directory. Lists information on 150,000+ U.S. companies.
Forbes Double 500 Directory. The directory of the 500 largest industrial corporations is published annually in May, and the directory of the 500 largest nonindustrial corporations is published each June.

If you don't mind getting mail and storing and organizing information, you can contact companies you have sent your resume to and ask for information, even before you are called for an interview. You may be able to pick up general information that may come in handy when you least expect it.

Job Leads

These resources list potential employers:

Job Hunters' Source Book
National Hotlines Directory
The National Jobline Directory

Periodicals And Articles

Don't neglect magazines, trade journals, and newsletters. Periodicals, both general and industry specific, can give you interesting and timely information about both industries and particular companies.

Your librarian can help you use the *Reader's Guide to Periodical Literature* to see if there have been recent articles about the company or about the industry you are interested in. Most libraries also have computerized search services that can make article-hunting fast and simple. Type in a keyword (like *IBM* or *health maintenance organizations*), and the software will find recent articles on such topics for you in its large databases.

Reading *Crain's, Newsweek, National Business Employment Weekly,* and your local newspaper will keep you current on industry news. You can scan articles quickly in your initial research phase.

Job Search Software

Check with your librarian to see what job search software is available for you to use in the library. Although CD-ROM products can be expensive, you may find that having such software available all the time at home is worth the investment. *Adam's JobBank* is available on CD-ROM, as are such titles as *American Big Business Directory, Dun and Bradstreet Middle Market Disc, Moody's Company Data,* and *Standard and Poor's Register.*

ADDITIONAL RESOURCES

The publications mentioned here will get you off to a good start, but there are many other resources available. You'll find a more comprehensive listing of such materials in Additional Resources at the end of this book.

The Telephone Book

Don't overlook your local telephone directory. It is easy to use and lists similar places of business under the same heading. Many cities have expanded business-to-business telephone directories that you can request from your local phone service provider.

Chamber of Commerce

Visit your local Chamber of Commerce. Ask whom you could speak to about local businesses. Since they're in the business of promoting businesses, they should be able to provide information about companies located in their area.

KEEP YOUR FOCUS AS YOU RESEARCH

The amount of information you'll have access to may seem overwhelming at times. Where do you begin? What, exactly are you looking for? Here's a three-step process for keeping your focus.

Step One

In order to be most efficient, you need to maintain your focus. Write your job objective here:

_____

Is there another name for this occupation?

_____

Step Two

List five types of employers who hire people for this kind of work.

_____

_____

_____

_____

_____

List two related occupations just in case you need to broaden your target market.

_____

_____

Step Three

Define your target market.

Size of company: _____

Geography: _____

Public or private: _____

Business, manufacturing, or service: _____

TARGETED MAILINGS

Once you have researched industries and located specific employers you are ready to begin your direct contact campaign. Targeted mailings are a good way to focus your job search and reach out to the companies in your area that hire people for the kinds of positions you are interested in.

Make a list of the industries and companies you are targeting. Prioritize that list and mail out around ten packets. Wait about ten days between mailings. If you are not getting responses after your follow-up calls, mail to your next set of targets. If you have selected an industry with few possibilities, you may want to expand your list.

Customize Your Cover Letters

You can start with the same basic cover letter, but customize each to include information gleaned from research. Make sure that you call to check names and direct your letters to specific parties. Choose something that you learned from your research and incorporate it into your letter. For example, you may have learned that the company has expanded its production by 300 percent or that the CEO just won an award for creating an educational incentive plan for employees. This information should go into paragraph two of your cover letter.

TRUE STORY

Research Pays Off

John was interested in a management position in a publicly held cosmetics company. He had completed his targeted direct mailing and had been called for an interview. Although he had some information about the company, he needed to learn more before the interview. He did the following:

- Called the company to request a copy of the annual report and any marketing brochures about product information
- Checked *Dun and Bradstreet* and *Standard and Poor's*
- Checked *Forbes Annual Report* and the *Directory of Directories* to learn about the cosmetics industry in general
- Searched the periodicals and found an article about the company's safe manufacturing record and its high level of customer product satisfaction
- Found a long article about the company's CEO in an association trade newsletter

John wowed them in his interview. He had invested a great deal of time and energy to learn about the company and it showed. He was offered a position, which he accepted.

Follow Up by Phone

Follow up each mailing with a phone call. In this era of phone mail and message menus, be persistent. You may have to call seven to ten times before you finally connect with the person you have been hoping to speak with. Prepare several phone scripts as follow up to your mailing (see Chapter 9 for advice about scripts). You will sound more natural and more confident if you take the time to practice out loud.

PHASE TWO: RESEARCH FOR AN INTERVIEW

Once you have been called for an interview, you will need to gather much more information very quickly. You can call the company and ask to get brochures, its annual report, copies of its internal newsletters, and any other public relations materials it has. Reviewing such information often reveals the culture of the company, its personnel, finances, and service or product trends.

Before your interview is the time to revisit the library and the *Readers' Guide to Periodical Literature* or its periodicals search software. Look for articles about your target industry and/or company. Reread thoroughly articles you may have skimmed before.

You may want to get information about a company's finances after you have been called for an interview. Companies teetering on the brink of financial collapse may be ripe for a takeover, which may mean that jobs may be insecure. You can obtain Securities and Exchange Commission Reports on publicly traded companies by writing to the Public References Section, Securities and Exchange Commission, Washington, DC 20549.

In Short

There's a job out there that is just right for you. Targeted direct contact allows you to reach those employers who hire people who do your type of work.

Remember:
- Establish your target
- Research the field
- Customize your mailings
- Follow up your mailing with a phone call
- Be persistent
- Research more thoroughly once you are called for an interview

Research Record

Company: _____

Contact Person: _____

Location: _____

Phone Number: _____

Fax Number: _____

Size/Number of Employees: _____

Ownership: _____

Products or Service: _____

Noteworthy Source: _____

_____

Other Important Information: _____

_____

Notes : _____

_____

_____

_____

_____

CHAPTER | 11

When job seeking, don't leave a stone unturned. In this chapter you'll learn about other useful job-seeking strategies: job fairs, help-wanted ads, placement agencies, school placement offices, business and professional associations, company hot-lines, and getting a foot in the door through voluntary work.

SEIZING OPPORTUNITIES
OTHER GOOD JOB-HUNTING METHODS

There are many different approaches you can use to make contact with employers besides networking and direct contact. As you read about these options in the following pages, think about your skills and the activities you enjoy and that you're best at. For example, if you like to write and are good at it, you may want to give developing customized cover letters in response to ads a high priority. If you're sociable and enjoy meeting new people, attending job fairs may be good for you. You'll find that a combination of strategies works best.

ANSWERING ADS

It is very tempting to rely on classified ads. They appear on set days in the newspaper and there are so many of them. Professional journals and trade papers also run position-open notices and ads on specific days. As easy as it may seem to send off a resume with a cover letter in response to some company's invitation to apply for an acknowledged opening, keep in mind that there are probably dozens, maybe even hundreds, of other people doing the same thing.

The competition for such announced job openings is keen. When an employer puts an ad in a newspaper, he is often inundated with responses. It is not uncommon for one ad to bring in 500 to 1,000 responses. No wonder employers prefer to fill jobs from personal referrals!

Customizing Your Responses

In order to strengthen your chances of turning ads into interviews, you must make sure that your personal advertising packet is appealing. Your cover letter must be concise, customized, creative, and correct. Your resume must be professional. Reread Chapters 6 and 7 on resumes and cover letters. Remember to:

- Customize your letter using key words from the ad
- Use the correct business letter format
- Use an 8 1/2-by-11 envelope to preserve the appearance of your resume packet

Follow up your mailing with a phone call. Be sure to save the ad. Make a copy of your cover letter and clip both to your Job Seeking Strategy Planning Record (JSSPR), located at the end of this chapter.

Sorting through Confusing Ad Categories

Newspaper classified advertisements may use different headings to list similar positions. In fact, on a recent Sunday, social work openings were found in a number of places in the classifieds—under "social work," "mental health," "case management," and "psychological services." Similarly, accounting positions were listed under "accounting," "accounts receivable," "fiscal manager," and "financial services." Keep in mind, if there are several help-wanted sections, you may have to read them all to be sure that you've found all the listings for your chosen field.

Practice

What is your target job?

_____

Can you think of five general titles where this type of work might be listed? Write them here:

_____

_____

_____

_____

_____

Check several papers and trade publications. Did you find any other titles listed for this type of position? If so, make note. Companies with big advertising budgets may take out larger advertisements that may be sprinkled throughout the help-wanted sections. Look for those in your field and read them carefully.

JOB FAIRS

Job fairs bring together employers from different industries, all under one roof. Sometimes as many as fifty companies participate, so these fairs are good opportunities for you to network and gather information. Employers are scouting for promising employees and you may have an impromptu interview on the spot. Important things to remember:

- **Dress for success.** Proper business attire is required. Even if a fair is on a weekend, don't go casual.
- **Take an ample supply of resumes.** Announcements often state the number of companies that will be at a fair, and you can use that number to calculate how many copies you may need. Better to take some back home with you than to run short. Place them in a professional-looking portfolio or briefcase. Crumpled or damp resumes in plastic bags do little to enhance your image!
- **Collect information and business cards from many employers.** Pick up material on any organization you're even remotely interested

in. Don't limit yourself at this time to just a few companies that look especially appealing to you. You may regret not having a card from some place that's later recommended to you, or that perhaps is opening up a new division, with new jobs available. It's a lot easier to throw away cards later than scramble to get them.

- **Take notes.** Carry a spare pen and a notebook and keep a record of company contacts and your impressions. Don't count on remembering information you didn't write down.

OPEN HOUSES AND CAREER FAIRS

In a recent Sunday edition of the *San Francisco Herald,* eight different companies announced that they were holding open houses. Each advertisement listed the departments and the titles of the advertised positions. For example, an insurance company was looking for underwriters, claims examiners, financial accountants, marketing reps, program analysts, and insurance trainees.

Career fairs and open houses mean that there are job openings now or will be in the near future. Open houses provide companies with an opportunity to collect resumes, to speak with and to either screen out or target potential employees. If you are unable to attend, most career fairs invite faxed resumes. In this case, you would customize a cover letter for each position that looks interesting.

Sometimes employment agencies organize closed job fairs on behalf of a particular employer. Read carefully. These announcements will specify that the agency will be screening resumes and will be setting up appointments for interviews at a later date with personnel from the sponsoring company. Research the company before responding so that you make a good impression in your cover letter.

COMPANY HOT LINES

Sometimes, large employers like big corporations, universities, and hospitals have phone-in hot lines where you can learn about job openings. Call directory assistance or the organizations' main phone numbers and ask.

TRUE STORY

Don't Limit Yourself Too Soon

A young man, relocating from Philadelphia to a small town on the New Jersey/Pennsylvania border, read about an open house for teachers in Newark, a city over 70 miles away from his new home. Although he did not want a long commute to work, he attended the fair because he was desperate. He'd sent out many resumes so far and had not gotten a single response.

He arrived dressed in work attire with a supply of resumes and was interviewed on the spot by a panel of interviewers, including the superintendent of schools from the county closest to his home. The next day, he followed up by calling to speak with the superintendent. He made it clear that he would take a teaching position in Newark in a second because he had no job, but what he *really* wanted was a job closer to home.

Two weeks later, the young man saw an ad for an English teacher in that superintendent's district in a school 12 miles away. He called the superintendent who, in turn, made a phone call to the school principal, a colleague of his, giving the young man a glowing recommendation. To make a long story short, the man is now teaching eighth grade English and has a 15-minute ride to work. It just goes to show: you never know what strategy or combination of methods can pay off.

PLACEMENT AGENCIES

Use the services of an employment agency *only* to supplement your own active search. Use their resources to learn information about a company or a field that's new to you, or perhaps to search job opportunities in a geographical area to which you're relocating. They can save you a lot of research time and effort.

There are two types of employment agencies: those to which you pay a fee and those paid by the employer. Many agencies work in all fields;

others specialize in particular industries such a health care or finance. When choosing an employment agency, you will want to know:

- How many years they have been in business
- Their placement rate
- The credentials of the placement professionals on staff

Temporary work through a temp agency can provide you with income while you are looking for a full-time job and help you make new networking contacts. Then there's a real possibility that a temporary position can turn into a full-time one.

GOVERNMENT EMPLOYMENT AGENCIES

Formerly called "unemployment offices," U.S. Department of Labor offices provide an enormous amount of information and assistance to job seekers, free of charge. Pamphlets and occupational guides for a variety of occupations explain the nature of the work, related occupations, key businesses that employ such workers, and the outlook for future employment. For other available publications, you may also write to: U.S. Department of Labor, Bureau of Labor Statistics, Office of Publications, Washington, DC 20212.

The U.S. Department of Labor maintains a nationwide database of job postings that can be accessed electronically. Counselors provide job-seeking tips and help in resume preparation as well. If you are receiving unemployment benefits, the U.S. Department of Labor may be able to refer you for retraining or for classes to upgrade your skills. These are free to eligible participants.

PUBLIC AGENCIES AND CIVIC ASSOCIATIONS

Many civic associations provide job information to targeted populations. Call local offices of agencies that promote economic development to check if employment counseling and services are available. Business and professional women's associations may have job services or provide useful networks for women job seekers. National and local groups for minorities often provide such services to their constituencies.

There are also state offices that serve individuals with disabilities who are seeking work. You can usually find such offices and agencies through your state education department. Phone hotlines are sometimes available.

SCHOOL PLACEMENT OFFICES

If you are a recent graduate or an alumnus of a college, you may be eligible for job search advice and referrals through the school's placement office. If you are at the beginning of your career, the kinds of positions that employers bring to college placement offices may be just right for you. Some colleges charge a nominal fee for services; others extend this service as a courtesy. These offices can provide good informational pamphlets and publications, and some have computers and software that you can use to prepare your resume and cover letters, and to access online services and electronic databases.

High school guidance counselors generally work with graduating seniors in their job searches. And since trade schools are vocationally oriented, it's not surprising to find that they generally offer job placement services for their graduates.

VOLUNTEER WORK

If you are thinking about a particular kind of work but have little experience in the field, you can make contact with a company, hospital, or service industry and offer to do voluntary work for them. Since you are involved in a job search, try to limit your volunteer experience to one day a week so that you'll have ample time for your real job: looking for a job. Although you won't get paid, volunteering can provide you with several very valuable benefits:

- An insider's view of the business or organization
- Real work experience for your resume
- Good references

KEEPING TRACK

Keeping a record of your activities is just as important as selecting appropriate strategies. If you are making good progress, you will be writing letters and thank you notes, calling contacts, attending information gathering meetings, going on interviews, doing research, handling the Internet—in short, doing so many things that your head will be spinning unless you keep good records.

THE PAPER WORK

There is paper work in all jobs. Since looking for work *is* your current job, you will need to keep accurate records. There are two simple ways to do this.

First, you can keep your networking contacts on index cards, as described in Chapter 9. This will enable you to see at a glance how one contact led to another. Since one of the keys to effective networking is "name dropping," you need to be sure to keep the connections straight.

Secondly, you can cross-reference these cards with brief notes on the Job Seeking Strategy Planning Record (JSSPR) at the end of this chapter. The JSSPR is designed to make it easy for you to keep and update detailed records. Here are the steps involved:

1. Get a large loose-leaf notebook.
2. Print up 150 copies of the JSSPR at the end of this chapter.
3. As you progress, copy information from index cards on the appropriate sheets. Also clip business cards and ads to the back of each day's record sheet.
4. Make copies of any correspondence that you mail. Be sure that all correspondence is dated.
5. Use copies of the Research Record form at the end of Chapter 10 to save your research notes. Office supply stores also carry loose-leaf pockets in which to keep pamphlets and other information that you collect.
6. Use sticky tags to mark days where follow-up action is needed.
7. Keep records of your job search expenses. Some, like child care, are tax deductible.

Complete and accurate records are essential. You do not want to find yourself in the position of the ill-prepared job seeker who went to an interview and asked, "What job is this anyway? I sent out so many resumes!"

IN SHORT

Now that you've know about the most effective traditional job-search techniques, perhaps you're ready to explore cyberspace and taking your search on-line in the next chapter. But before you do, let's recap a bit. Remember:

- Networking and direct contact are most effective job-hunting strategies.
- Use only four different strategies at a time so that you don't spread yourself too thin.
- Maintain accurate and complete records of your activities.

JOB SEEKING STRATEGY PLANNING RECORD
(JSSPR)

Research: **Date_____**

Company	Contact	Address	Phone	Action

Met with:

Contact	Phone	Referral to	Action

Wrote to:

Contact	Company	Notes/Action	Follow Up

Called:

Contact/Number	Company	Notes/Action	Follow Up

Follow Up Needed (use sticky tags for timely reminders)

Call: _____

Write to: _____

Meet with: _____

Expenses incurred:

_____

_____

_____

_____

CHAPTER | 12

Cyberspace, here you come! This chapter will get you started on exploring job opportunities in a brand new territory: the Internet. You'll get the basics of the Internet, and then find out about key Web sites for job hunters. Finally you'll discover how to search for the Web sites of Fortune 500 companies to read about their histories and possible job opportunities.

SURFING FOR JOBS
THE INTERNET JOB SEARCH

In order to do on-line searches for employment opportunities, you must first understand how to get around on the Internet. Let's start with the World Wide Web, a graphical, easy-to-use system on the Internet that offers the user a vast amount of information. The Web is a huge collection of documents called Web pages that are designed to be user-friendly.

Even if you've never been on-line before, you'll have no problem following the on-screen instructions. Web pages present information in various forms; there are graphics, words, sounds, and sometimes even video clips.

WEB BASICS

The acronym for the World Wide Web is WWW, or the Web. Web *browsers,* such as Netscape Navigator and Microsoft Explorer, are programs that help you explore information on the Web. *Hypertext* is text that contains links to other pages on the Web. By double clicking using your mouse, you can select hypertext and jump from one page to another.

EXPLORE THE WEB

When exploring the Web, you can view pages stored on computers around the world. A Web browser keeps track of all the Web sites you visit along the way. The home page is the first page you see when you start you trip. Exploring the Web is easier if you use a search engine, and there are many to choose from, including Yahoo!, AltaVista, Lycos, and Excite. The search engines are free services and can be located by simply entering a specific address: *www.yahoo.com/,* for example.

A search engine is similar to having a tour guide in a foreign country. Search engines allow you to explore the Web by simply typing in a category or word. You type in a word or a descriptive phrase and the search engine explores the Internet, looking for information relating to the topic. It brings you a list of Web sites that contain the information you are trying to find.

Searching for Job Opportunities

If you're looking for a job, the Internet is one of your most valuable tools. You can search the Net in two ways:

1. Use a search engine by typing in words like "Employment Opportunities" or "Jobs." (But be forewarned: using such general terms like these will generate a lot of entries; typing in a particular job category will help narrow your search.)
2. Go directly to Web sites that are designed to locate available employment.

Using a search engine to find employment will generate a list of Web sites that have employment lists or anything related to employment opportunities. Because the Web is worldwide, some of the information will be about employment in other countries. You may have to view a few of the sites to determine which best fit your needs.

JOB SITES ON THE WEB

Below is a list of employment opportunity Web sites available by directly entering the World Wide Web address for each. If you see *http://* already listed on your screen, then begin by typing *www.* Don't leave spaces between the sections of the address. If a message comes up saying that the server can't find your address, then check your spelling and make sure you haven't added a space between sections of the address. Also make sure you've entered a period (.) and not a comma (,)—or the search engine can't find your entry.

POSTING YOUR RESUME ON SITES

Several Web sites have areas where you can post your resume, which is very easy to do. Each site comes with a set of directives. Basically, it involves typing your name, address, phone, and E-mail address, and then pasting a copy of your resume in the appropriate area. The only drawback of putting your resume on the Internet is that the information is not protected. This means anyone can read your resume and use the information for things other than employment opportunities. You may want to consider supplying your E-mail address instead of your home address and phone number.

Although posting your resume may not be the most effective method for circulating your resume, it can be one part of your general networking strategies. As Internet use becomes more popular among businesses, more employers may use it to search for potential employees.

Web Sites

The following sites are very active, so it may take time to gain access to them:

The AT&T College Network *http://www.att.com./college/*
This is a one-stop shopping center. You can search for all kinds of jobs located all over the world. There is also career-related information. Go to the job search engine and tailor your search to the type of job you want, the company, or the geographic area. There are lots of other

useful sections on this address. Listings are frequently updated. This site will also lead you to many other Web sites.

Career Mosaic *http://www.careermosiac.com/*

This site lists job openings and information about companies like Intel and many others. You can also get dates and locations of upcoming job fairs or post your resume at the site and wait for offers.

The Monster Board *http://www.monster.com/*

Its name says it all: it's got a wide range of job postings from top companies. One of the first on-line career sites, it's also one of the largest. Look in the Jobs in Paradise section for unusual entry-level jobs.

Big Yellow.com *http://www/bigyellow.com/*

Let your fingers do the typing. Search from among more than 16 million U.S. business listings.

Commerce Park *http://www.commercepark.com/*

This is a great site for large or small business owners and entrepreneurs who want to exchange information, make connections, and conduct business on-line.

Career Path.com *http://www.careerpath.com/*

Search newspapers all over the country for new jobs at this site. With monthly updates, you can also register here to have job information E-mailed directly to you. Search the classified ads for the last two Sundays of the *New York Times,* which are upgraded every Saturday evening. View them before the paper is sent to the public, giving you a jumpstart over other job searchers.

E-Span *http://www.espan.com/*

This site matches job profiles against vacancies at 2,000 companies.

Job Bank USA *http://www.jobbankusa.com/*

The Job Bank stores resumes and does job searches.

SEARCH FORTUNE 500 COMPANIES

As you know by now, having information about a company is a necessity when you go for an interview. The information definitely gives you an edge over other candidates. Today that search is simplified by the Internet. For example, if you were going on a job interview with a company such as Lucent Technologies, you would simply type in the address of the company and its Web site appears on your screen. Most company addresses are simply the name of the company. Lucent Technologies, for example, is *http://www.lucent.com/*.

Most large companies and even many small companies have Web sites. If the Web address isn't the company name, just go to a search engine such as AltaVista, and type in the company name, such as "Lucent Technologies."

Searching Web sites of large companies can sometimes lead to job opportunities because many of them post job opportunities and job openings right on their Web sites.

TRUE STORY

The Internet to the Rescue

Adam was frustrated in his job search and was feeling desperate. On Sunday, he bought the newspaper and cut out all the advertisements he could find for work in a health care agency. Then he wrote cover letters specific for each of the ads. He mailed and faxed his resume and cover letters out to the companies he found listed.

On Wednesday, National Healthcare called him and scheduled an interview for Friday. He didn't know anything about the company, so he went to the library and signed up for Internet time. He looked under *www.yahoo.com* and found National Healthcare. On its home page he found a description of the company, which was newly created by the merger of two health care giants. There were also press releases, articles about the CEO, and names of other directories for additional information.

Adam made a printout and reviewed it before he met with the director of human resources. He impressed the director with his knowledge of National Healthcare's history, personnel, and operations. He was offered a second interview on the spot.

IN SHORT

A wealth of information is at your fingertips when you master the Internet. You can use it to:

- Circulate your resume
- Search for job postings
- Quickly gather vast amounts of information about companies

CHAPTER | 13

Filling out forms without making mistakes requires care, concentration, and attention to directions. The advice in this chapter will ensure that your job applications are neat, correct, and ready to make a good first impression.

THE DREADED JOB APPLICATION
HOW TO COPE

A job application—you can obtain it in one of two ways. You can walk into a company's personnel office "cold" and ask the secretary for an application. You fill it out and leave. The directions on the application may ask that you attach a copy of your resume. In this case, your application is a screening device. Sloppy applications never make it past the secretary's desk to the next level of review. Since there are usually many applicants for the same job, your paperwork must stand out if it is to be forwarded on.

The other way of getting an application is to be given one from an employer. Someone in the position of hiring has some interest in you as a potential employee and wants to know more about you, so he asks you to fill out a comprehensive application, which may precede an interview. If you are lucky, the longer form will arrive by mail so that you can fill it out in the leisure of your home.

IMPORTANT THINGS TO KNOW ABOUT APPLICATIONS

Last name first, first name last! Do *not* pick up your pen to fill out a job application until you read this *entire* chapter because:

- Applications often look easy but they're not.
- They ask for a great deal of information in very small spaces.
- All applications ask for similar information but in a different order.
- You must follow directions very carefully.
- It's essential that applications be neat and complete.
- Often you are filling out an application in a busy personnel office where it is easy to become distracted.

ADVANCE PREPARATION

Applications always call for personal, educational, and job data. The easiest and most efficient way to fill out an application is to have this information at your fingertips.

EDUCATIONAL INFORMATION

Think carefully about your educational history. Make a list that includes:

- Name and location of each school and training program that you attended
- Dates of attendance
- Exact name of certificate or degree
- Number of credits attained

Transfer this information to an index card.

EMPLOYMENT HISTORY

Next, make a list of all the jobs you have held. Include:

- Full name of company and its location
- Job title
- Dates of service—be as specific as possible; some applications call for month and year

- Brief description of duties
- Name and title of your supervisor
- Reason for leaving
- Salary

Put this information on another index card.

OTHER INFORMATION YOU MAY NEED

If you hold licensure in a particular profession, look for the exact name of the license and your license number, and put this information on another index card. If you are not a United States citizen, write down your visa ID number. Be sure to note the date of expiration.

If you have followed these directions, you now have concise, accurate information on index cards that you can transfer to job applications when you're out in the field or to use when filling them out at home.

DOCUMENTS TO HAVE READY

Sometimes, you may be asked to attach documentation to an application. Be sure to have copies of:

- Your resume
- Your high school or college diploma or GED
- An official transcript of your credits
- Any certificates, awards for specialized training, continuing education transcripts, or state or national licenses or credentials you may hold (for instance, licensed electrician, physical therapy assistant, alcoholism counselor, certified dietary manager, NACLES certified phlebotomist, or whatever)

Since it may take several weeks to accumulate this information, you should begin the process as soon as you initiate your job search. Make sure that you have ample copies of each so that you do not have to give away your original. Once you get a job offer, you may need to submit the originals.

FILLING OUT APPLICATIONS

Once you have prepared your information and have it written on index cards, you are ready to begin to fill out applications. When in the field, you will need to carry your prepared information and documents. Purchase a business portfolio to keep papers clean and safe.

COMPLETING APPLICATIONS AT HOME

It is always easier to complete an application at home because you can practice. Before you pick up your pen, make a copy of the application and fill it out. After you have double-checked that the copy is accurate and complete, carefully transfer the information to the original. If you can, ask someone else to check your work before you transfer the information to the actual application you will submit.

IMPORTANT TIPS

Here are some tips on filling out applications, whether at home or in a personnel office:

- Don't leave home without your index cards. Read the entire application *before* picking up a pen.
- Note whether information is requested in chronological or in reverse order.
- Work slowly and carefully.
- Use your full name—no nicknames please.
- If you have worked or hold licensure under your maiden name, make note of that on your application.
- Use blue or black ink, unless pencil is specified.
- Use an erasable pen, just in case.
- Answer all questions truthfully. If a question does not apply to your experience, write *not applicable, NA,* or *does not apply* to let the reader know that you have paid attention to all questions.
- Check your work before handing it in.
- Bring paper clips or a small stapler along with your documents in case an attachment is called for.

Practice

At the end of this chapter you will find two applications. The first one is blank. Make a photocopy of this blank application, then read the directions for the application carefully and fill out this copy. When you have finished, look it over to see if there are sections that you crossed out or erased. You will need to pay special attention to that data area when you fill out other job applications.

Now, check to see how your work compares with the second, filled-in application here for your review. If you made mistakes, complete the blank application in the book, paying special attention to any area that gave you trouble the first time.

Neat and accurate applications make a good impression. Take the extra time to give yourself ample opportunities for practice. Make the rounds of local area banks, schools, or fast food eateries. Ask for employment applications and take them home. Fill them out carefully and when you are done, double-check or ask a friend to double-check for you. These may be different from the ones included in this book.

- If you find that any of these practice applications ask for any information that is not on your index cards, add it to your cards, because you may find that such information is needed on actual applications you fill out.
- Is there an area that consistently gives you trouble? Use a highlighter to call your attention to this area. Pay special attention when similar information is called for the next time.

IN SHORT

Now that you have completed this chapter, you are ready to tackle "real" applications in personnel offices. Remember:
- Prepare your information cards and bring them with you.
- Read directions carefully.
- Do not pick up your pen until you have read the *entire* application.

Your application is the first impression you give to a potential employer. Make sure that it is a good one.

WEST PALM BEACH UNIVERSITY HOSPITAL
3133 EXETER PARKWAY
WEST PALM BEACH, FLORIDA 33120

Personal Information:

Referred by: _____

Name in Full _____

Last   First   Middle

Home Address _____

No.   Street   Apt. #   City   State   Zip

Telephone Number ( )_____ ( )_____

Home   Business   S.S. No.

Are you authorized to work in the U.S.? Yes_____ No_____

Visa Number: _____ Date of Expiration: _____

Are you below the age of 18? ☐ Yes ☐ No

If YES, indicate date of birth _____ Month _____ Day _____ Year

Position Desired:

Other positions you qualify for:

RECORD OF EDUCATION

Circle highest grade completed:

High School 9 10 11 12 College 1 2 3 4

Graduate School 1 2 3 4 Degree or Major _____

Salary Desired _____ Minimum Salary you will accept _____

Type of position desired ☐ Permanent ☐ Full-Time
                        ☐ Temporary ☐ Part-Time ☐ Per Diem

If temporary, how long: _____

Circle days of week available

Sat   Sun   Mon   Tue   Wed   Thurs   Fri

Hours available: From _____ AM To _____ AM
                              PM   PM

Shifts you will work: ☐ Day ☐ Evening ☐ Night ☐ All

	Name of School	Did you graduate?
High School		
College		
Other training		

Please note: If you are applying for a position which requires a high school diploma, GED, undergraduate or graduate degree, you will be required to submit the original document as well as an official transcript before final acceptance for the position.

GED: Year Issued _____   Certificate #: _____

LICENSURE

License	Issuing Authority	Certificate Number	Expiration Date

Have you ever had a license suspended or revoked? _____ Yes _____ No   If yes, give full details.

EMPLOYMENT HISTORY: Begin with present or last job and work back for the last years. Attach an extra page, if necessary.

1. Firm Name: _____   Address _____

   Dates Employed From ____ / ____   To ____ / ____   Job Title _____
                        Mo.   Yr.   Mo.   Yr.

   Final Base Salary/indicate <u>one</u>

   ( ) Annual $ _____
   ( ) Weekly $ _____
   ( ) Hourly $ _____

   Name and Title of
   Immediate Supervisor _____   Reason for Leaving _____

   Briefly describe duties _____
   _____
   _____
   _____

2. Firm Name: _____   Address _____

   Dates Employed From ____ / ____   To ____ / ____   Job Title _____
                        Mo.   Yr.   Mo.   Yr.

   Final Base Salary/indicate <u>one</u>

   ( ) Annual $ _____
   ( ) Weekly $ _____
   ( ) Hourly $ _____

Name and Title of
Immediate Supervisor _____ Reason for Leaving _____

Briefly describe duties _____
_____
_____

3. Firm Name: _____ Address _____
    Dates Employed From ___/___ To ___/___   Job Title _____
                     Mo. Yr.   Mo. Yr.   Final Base Salary/indicate one
                                                            ( ) Annual $
                                                            ( ) Weekly $
                                                            ( ) Hourly $

Name and Title of
Immediate Supervisor _____ Reason for Leaving _____

Briefly describe duties _____
_____
_____

Signature: _____   Date: _____

WEST PALM BEACH UNIVERSITY HOSPITAL
3133 EXETER PARKWAY
WEST PALM BEACH, FLORIDA 33120

Personal Information: Referred by: _Janice Darby_

Name in Full _Gesbin_ _Gloria_ _Haily_
              Last   First   Middle

Home Address _419 Cebra Ave_ _2L_ _Brooklyn_ _N.Y._ _11206_
             No. Street   Apt. # City   State   Zip

Telephone Number (_718_) _432-1090_ ( ) _N/A_   _167-23-5482_
                 Home   Business   S.S. No.

Are you authorized to work in the U.S.? Yes _✓_ No ____

Visa Number: _N/A_   Date of Expiration: _N/A_

Are you below the age of 18? ☐ Yes
                             ☒ No

If YES, indicate date of birth ____ Month ____ Day ____ Year

Position Desired: _Patient Care Associate_

Other positions you qualify for: _Ward Clerk_

RECORD OF EDUCATION

Circle highest grade completed:

High School 9 10 11 (12) College 1 (2) 3 4

Graduate School 1 2 3 4   Degree or Major _____

Salary Desired **open** Minimum Salary you will accept $ **10/HR**

Type of position desired [☑] Permanent [☑] Full-Time

[ ] Temporary [ ] Part-Time [ ] Per Diem

If temporary, how long: _____

Circle days of week available

(Sat) (Sun) (Mon) (Tue) (Wed) (Thurs) (Fri)

Hours available: From __7__ (AM)/PM To __8__ AM/(PM)

Shifts you will work: [☑] Day [ ] Evening [ ] Night [ ] All

	Name of School	Did you graduate?
High School	williams H.S.	Yes
College	NYU	No
Other training	mandel school	Yes

Please note: If you are applying for a position which requires a high school diploma, GED, undergraduate or graduate degree, you will be required to submit the original document as well as an official transcript before final acceptance for the position.

GED: Year Issued _____ Certificate #: _____

LICENSURE

License	Issuing Authority	Certificate Number	Expiration Date
Certified Nurse Aide	N.Y.S.	100-429 b	2/1/99

Have you ever had a license suspended or revoked? _____ Yes __✓__ No   If yes, give full details.

EMPLOYMENT HISTORY: Begin with present or last job and work back for the last years. Attach an extra page, if necessary.

1. Firm Name: _Brooklyn Hospital_   Address _486 Brooklyn Ave   Brooklyn, NY_

   Dates Employed From _9_ / _96_ To _6_ / _97_   Job Title _Patient Care_   Final Base Salary/indicate one
            Mo.   Yr.   Mo.   Yr.   _Associate_
                                            ( ) Annual $ _____
                                            ( ) Weekly $ _____
                                            (✓) Hourly $ _9.50_

   Name and Title of
   Immediate Supervisor _Brenda Lockert_
                  Nursing Supervisor   Reason for Leaving _relocating_

   Briefly describe duties _Assisted with ADL, took EKG examinations, drew blood_
   specimens, accurately took vital signs and charted findings, assisted
   medical care team.

2. Firm Name: _Crown Nursing Home_   Address _81 Kings Highway Brooklyn, NY_

   Dates Employed From _8_ / _94_ To _8_ / _96_   Job Title _Nurse Aide_   Final Base Salary/indicate one
            Mo.   Yr.   Mo.   Yr.
                                            ( ) Annual $ _____
                                            ( ) Weekly $ _____
                                            (✓) Hourly $ _8.00_

Name and Title of John Jenkins

Immediate Supervisor Patient Care Supervisor Reason for Leaving Job Advancement

Briefly describe duties Assisted chronically ill patients with ADL, accompanied
patients for test procedures, maintained skin care to prevent ulcers,
worked as part of team implementing doctors' instructions

3. Firm Name: St. Savior Hospital   Address 471 8th Street Brooklyn, NY

Dates Employed From 9 / 93 To 7 / 94   Job Title Clerk, receptionist   Final Base Salary/indicate one

    Mo. Yr.   Mo. Yr.

( ) Annual $
( ) Weekly $
(✓) Hourly $ 7.00

Name and Title of Alice Rumpell

Immediate Supervisor Director of Personnel   Reason for Leaving Graduated from high school
Job Advancement

Briefly describe duties Maintained index of patient rooms, greeted visitors and
directed them to patient floors, worked as clerk in gift shop,
handled computerized cash register, stocked shelves in shop.

Signature: Gloria Glabin   Date: 1/3/97

CHAPTER | 14

Understanding the employer's goals is key to a good interview. In order to market yourself in a convincing and appropriate way, you have to know what the interviewer wants. But you also have to know what you want. In this chapter you'll learn how to get a handle on your interviewer's needs and ask the questions that will get you the answers you need to know about the job and the company.

BEFORE THE INTERVIEW
PREPARATION

An interview is an opportunity for you to sell yourself. This doesn't mean sell just your skills, expertise, and experience, but also your unique personality. *You* are the product that this company is considering buying. Obviously you have some of the job-specific skills that the employer is seeking or he would not have called you to interview for the position. But he's not just looking for a person to carry out the responsibilities of the job. He's also looking for an individual who can blend in and become an important part of the team.

A company is not hiring your resume; it's hiring you. It's not necessarily the most qualified candidate who gets the position; it's the one with whom the interviewer feels most comfortable and in whom he has the most confidence.

THE EMPLOYER'S INTERVIEW GOALS

First and foremost, an employer is looking for someone with a good work ethic and a positive attitude. He's looking for a team player who is willing to learn new things, who's flexible, loyal, honest, enthusiastic, organized, and decisive. He wants a person who can fit into his workplace "family" and can communicate with clients and staff—someone who will contribute to the organization's growth.

Does this sound like you? Of course it does! Now it's up to you to convince the employer during your interview that you are the right person for the job.

YOUR INTERVIEW GOALS

You've got two main goals:

1. To convince the interviewer that you're the right person for the job.

2. To learn first hand about the job and the organization itself.

Achieving the first goal has to do with how you answer the interview questions and the impression you make on the employer. You'll read more about these later, in this chapter and in the next two chapters.

As for the second, remember that it's a two-way interview: theirs *and yours.* The research you do about the company before your interview (see Do Your Homework, later in this chapter) will only tell you the facts about this employer. Your interview gives you the opportunity to learn first-hand about the organization's "personality" and about its goals. The person doing the interview will ask you questions, and you'll also have the opportunity to ask some of your own. (See Chapter 15 for the types of questions you may be asked and those you will want to ask yourself.)

After the interview, you might be offered the job. If so, congratulations! They want you. But before accepting, be certain *you* want *them.* The answers to your questions during the interview should have told you a lot about the job and the company—enough to make the right decision.

THE PRE-INTERVIEW

Some large companies screen candidates on the phone before they ask them to come in for a face-to-face interview. This pre-interview can determine if an applicant's basic skills, values, and ethics match the profile of their ideal employee.

The company will notify you before the phone interview as to the day and time they will be calling you. This pre-interview can be very short, or it can take up to 45 minutes or so. It's a good idea to ask the person who calls to set it up how long you should expect it to take. The interviewer will ask you questions and record your answers.

Here are some of the kinds of questions you might be asked in a phone interview:

- Do you think it is ever right to bend the truth?
- How do you feel about the statement, "It's not my job"?
- How do you feel about someone who works only for the money, the paycheck?
- Do you feel a need to achieve something every day? If yes, tell me what you have achieved in the last two days.

Don't worry about such a pre-interview, just answer the questions truthfully. There's absolutely nothing you can do to prepare for it except to be there when the call comes in and be yourself.

THE INTERVIEWER

Who conducts the in-person interview generally depends on the size of the organization and its structure. Generally, small companies don't have a centralized hiring system; you're interviewed by the owner or manager. Usually only large companies have personnel or human resource offices. These departments screen applicants and make hiring decisions for entry-level positions. Sometimes they narrow the field to three or four applicants who they've interviewed by phone or in person, and then these candidates are interviewed again by a supervisor, department head, or perhaps even a team of people.

So, you can see that you might be interviewed by someone who has limited experience as an employment specialist, someone who has a great deal of experience, or a person somewhere in between. A novice is more likely to ask you the routine questions to determine if the information and skills you listed on your resume are accurate. A real professional will probably ask you those and some more challenging questions. (You'll see a whole range of possible questions later, in Chapter 15).

WHAT TO DO BEFORE THE INTERVIEW

The interview is your opportunity to market yourself to this employer. You need to answer his questions to your advantage. So you should be prepared to talk about your abilities, to "toot your own horn." In order to keep the conversation flowing with information about yourself, here's what you should do ahead of time:

- Make a list of your strongest skills and work-related characteristics and review them several times until you know them off the top of your head.
- Think of concrete examples from work or school to prove you've got these skills and assets. Review them several times.
- Anticipate questions about the information on your resume.
- Be prepared to defend your strengths as well as your weaknesses.
- Be ready to tell the interviewer what *you* want him to know about you.
- Practice talking about yourself so that you're comfortable doing it in an interview.

PREPARE A PORTFOLIO

There are jobs in certain fields in which a work portfolio can be a real asset. Graphic artists, fashion designers, and photographers are obvious examples. But there are others as well: a job in architecture or blueprint making, or one that involves writing. In fact, for almost any job, if you can provide an actual specimen of your work, then a portfolio can be an effective way to showcase your talents and experience.

A portfolio must be carefully prepared and make a very good first impression. It should include a *small* selection of your best work, along with newspaper articles or reviews about you and your work; complimentary letters from clients or previous employers; and any awards you might have won at school, through your community, or from a trade or professional organization.

The portfolio represents your talents, so make sure it is attractive and represents you at your best.

DO YOUR HOMEWORK

Don't go to an interview without reviewing the job advertisement (if there is one), as well as all the information you have researched about the company and the position you're interested in.

Employers are always impressed when job candidates know something about their company and can speak about it with some degree of familiarity. If you can, then you'll come across as someone who's seriously interested in the organization and in being a part of it. How would you feel as an employer if a candidate didn't know what position he was interviewing for?

TRUE STORY

What Company *Is* This Anyway?
During an interview for an administrative assistant position, a candidate was asked, "Why do you want this job?" Her response was, "I sent out so many resumes, I don't remember what job this is." What would *you* do if you were the interviewer? Explain the job and give her a copy of the job ad to refresh her memory, eliminate her from consideration, or appreciate her candor and bring her in for a second interview?

The applicant was given a copy of the advertisement to read, had the job described to her, and was interviewed. However, she was also eliminated from consideration for the position.

KNOW WHERE YOU'RE GOING

Make sure you know the correct address, floor, and room number where you will be interviewed. Get instructions on how to get to the interview site. If you're nervous or unsure about how to get there, then try out the instructions by actually making the trip beforehand. Be sure to call and confirm your appointment at least the day before. Leave nothing to the last minute. Plan on being *early*—15–20 minutes is about right.

If you are ill the day of the interview, call and reschedule. Do not go to your interview if you are sick; you can't sell yourself effectively if you are not feeling well.

DRESS APPROPRIATELY

Unless you are auditioning to be a rock star, dress conservatively. First impressions count. To get you thinking, try picking the appropriate attire from the following:

Women:
    a. A mini skirt with a long blazer, high heels, and large hoop earrings
    b. A tailored suit with low- or mid-heeled shoes, a simple necklace, and earrings
    c. Jeans with a sweater and low shoes

Men:
    a. A pair of blue jeans with a white shirt, sports jacket, and loafers
    b. A suit with a white shirt, tie, and dress shoes
    c. Sweatpants with a tee-shirt and sneakers

The correct answer is **b** for both men and women. Actors put their costumes on before they go on stage. Business attire is the appropriate costume for an interview. Your interviewing outfit should be:

- Men: A dark suit, white shirt, tie, knee length socks, dark oxford shoes.
- Women: Conservative blouse and suit, with skirt not too short, sensible heels, subtle makeup and jewelry. Fill only one hole with earrings if you have many.

TRUE STORY

Clothes Make the Man—or Woman

The field was narrowed down to two candidates for the position as a counselor in a job-training program. One candidate was a mature woman with lots of credentials and experience. The other was a new college graduate with a degree but only internship experience to her credit.

For the last interview, the mature candidate showed up in a sheer blouse inappropriate for work. The young graduate had on a tailored, classic navy blue suit; she looked very professional. "She looked like Miss America," one of her interviewers remarked afterward. The young graduate got the job despite her lack of paid experience.

APPEARANCE COUNTS

If you don't own any clothing that is appropriate, then buy an interviewing outfit. It doesn't have to be expensive, but it should look neat and well made, and it should fit you well. If you are asked back for a second interview, you can wear the same suit again. If you're a woman, you can change your blouse and accessories, and, if a man, change your tie and shirt.

Consider the expense as an investment in your future. Once you're dressed and ready to go to your interview, you don't want to give your appearance a second thought. You know you're putting your best foot forward. Concentrate on the important part: selling yourself to the employer.

Employers set the rules. After all, it's their job. Appearances count and first impressions are lasting ones. Remember, there's plenty of time to dye that purple stripe back into your hair again once your new employer appreciates you for your many talents.

TRUE STORY

First Impressions Make All the Difference

A male candidate had all the qualifications and expertise for the job. He was nicely dressed and exuded confidence. While he waited to be interviewed, he was pleasant and friendly to the receptionist. The interview went extremely well. Unfortunately, he did not get the job.

Looking for a clue as to what went wrong during the interview so that he could avoid making the same mistake in the future, he called the receptionist and asked her why she thought he didn't get the job. "They loved you," she told him, "but they just weren't comfortable with your beard."

Several months later another position at the company was advertised. This time the applicant shaved his beard off, and he landed the job. A year later, when he had become a valued member of the department, he grew his beard back.

STANDARDS OF APPEARANCE

You want the first impression that you make on a future employer to be a positive one. The following are accepted standards in the job market. Follow them if you want to make a positive first impression.

Women:

- Don't wear your skirts too short or too tight, heels too high, or blouses too low and too sheer.
- Skip the loud nail colors and long nails. Keep your makeup subtle.
- Carry an extra pair of stockings just in case and wear them, even in the summer.
- Don't wear too much jewelry; keep it simple. Don't wear lots of earrings.

Men:

- Don't wear an earring.
- Keep your nails clean and trimmed and always remember to shave.
- Wear knee length socks that match your pants to avoid "the sock gap."

Everyone:

- If you think you might need a haircut, get one.
- Don't splash on too much perfume or aftershave. Many people are allergic to scents.
- Don't wear a nose ring.
- Take a shower that morning and wear a deodorant.
- Polish your shoes and press your clothes the night before.
- Absolutely don't chew gum or smoke.
- If you suffer from sweaty palms, keep a handkerchief with a *little* baby powder or cornstarch in it. Before your interview, go into the restroom and dry your hands with it.
- Go to the interview alone. Don't bring a friend or relative.
- Get a good night's sleep the night before.

WHAT TO BRING TO THE INTERVIEW

Bring a few copies of your resume, just in case. Also take a small notebook and pen to jot down the names, correct titles, and addresses of those who interview you. You will need this information for your post-interview thank-you notes. The notebook is also handy for writing down answers to questions you ask during the interview or for remembering any additional materials interviewers might ask you to send them. Bring a list of any questions you have so that you don't forget to ask them.

In addition, bring the names, addresses, and telephone numbers of three individuals who have agreed to be your personal and professional references. Take any documents you may need for the interview, such as your social security card or driver's license. You can carry all these items in any appropriate folder or case that you own.

A FINAL CHECK

Since you will be arriving early to your interview, you will have plenty of time to go into the restroom and check yourself over. Brush or comb your hair. Men, straighten your tie. Ladies, freshen your lipstick. Give yourself the once over, take a deep breath and exhale several times, and then smile in the mirror. No one but you should know about the butterflies fluttering in your stomach!

IN SHORT

Here are the things you need to do before your interview:
- Review your list of skills and characteristics
- Know where your interview is taking place and confirm the date and time.
- Have your interviewing outfit ready; be sure to try it on beforehand.
- Take extra copies of your resume and your questions with you.
- Bring a small pen and notebook.

You will also want to be familiar with the types of questions you may be asked and have concise and convincing answers ready. In the next chapter you'll have a chance to review sample questions an interviewer may ask you, as well as the ones you can ask the interviewer. Then you'll put it all to the test in Chapter 16.

CHAPTER | 15

In this chapter you will review possible questions you may be asked in an interview and get advice on how to answer them; find out which questions are legal and which are illegal to ask; and prepare the types of questions *you* can ask.

INTERVIEW QUESTIONS
THEIRS AND YOURS

If you were shopping for a car, you'd spend a lot of time in different dealerships asking lots of questions. You would decide the features that you absolutely wanted and then you would compare makes and models and how much they cost. Only after careful consideration would you finally decide which one to buy.

An interviewer has the same challenges when she shops for an employee. During an interview, she's evaluating all the information you're telling her so that she can compare you to the other applicants.

MARKET YOURSELF

The interviewer must determine if you're the right candidate for the job, if you've got what it takes to be valuable member of her team. Like a careful car buyer she will ask lots of questions to see if you have the skills, ability, and personality for the job. That's why preparing for the interview and learning how to "market" yourself is so important.

Some people find it difficult to talk about themselves. But an interview is one of the few times that it's acceptable to brag about your accomplishments, so long as you do it in an appropriate way. Never answer a question with a simple yes or no. Use each question to tell the interviewer more about your skills and accomplishments, and when possible, give concrete examples to demonstrate them.

LISTEN CAREFULLY

You'll really find out about the job requirements during the interview. Listen carefully to the things your interviewer tells you about the company and the position. You'll pick up information that you can use to your advantage. Perhaps she's mentioned a lack of organization on the part of the employee who previously had the position for which you're interviewing. Your answer should stress your organizational skills and give specific examples of them. The work environment, personality of your interviewer, and what she says about the company or the department should give you good clues about the company. Bring out those strengths and characteristics in you that you think will be valued there. Every company has an image of the "perfect" employee. You want to fit that image.

QUESTIONS INTERVIEWERS OFTEN ASK

Below you'll find a sample of general questions that employers often ask candidates. Prepare an answer for these and you'll be ready to answer them, or any variation on them.

About yourself:
- What can you tell me about yourself?
- What are your strengths?
- What are your weaknesses/failures?
- Describe your long- and short-range goals.

Business questions:
- Why do you want to work here?
- What special qualities do you bring to this job?
- What was your worst job?
- Discuss a problem you have had at work/with your boss (or coworker) and how you resolved it.
- How do you define success?
- What are your strengths, your weaknesses/failures?
- Where do you see yourself, careerwise, in the future?

School questions:
- Do you think your school grades represent you?
- What was the main thing you got out of going to college (high school)?
- Why didn't you get a degree?
- How did your education prepare you for a career?
- What did you learn in school that can help you on the job?

And finally:
- Is there anything else I need to know about you?
- Do you have any questions?

An interviewer might also ask you to:
- Explain or defend any statement you made in your resume.
- Discuss any skill you may have listed.
- Discuss any lapses in employment times.

SAMPLE ANSWERS TO QUESTIONS OFTEN ASKED

No two interviewers will ask all the same questions. The ones you just reviewed are only a few of many. Each question can be asked in more than one way. Take the time to prepare your own personalized responses to them. The following answers are only meant to serve as guides for you.

QUESTION: "TELL ME ABOUT YOURSELF"

Interviewers often begin with a broad question like "Tell me about yourself." If asked this question, don't talk about every job you ever had. Take this opportunity to explain your skills and special abilities. Target your answer so that your expertise matches the employer's needs. Start with broad strokes and, as you continue during the interview, add the details. Script out your answer ahead of time. Take the time to really develop it. Be prepared to "toot your own horn."

Sample Answer

"I've always been one of those people who could fix anything. As a child, I could take things apart and put them back together. My parents bought a computer for our family when I was 12. It wasn't long before I became the neighborhood computer whiz, helping everyone with their problems. I was just 16 when I started working part time for a local computer store. By the time I was 18, I was an assistant manager. I developed business management expertise on the job. By the time I started college, I was responsible for hiring and training both technical and nontechnical employees.

"In college, I maintained a 4.0 average in both my computer science major and business minor. I'm proud of both my technical expertise and my ability to manage a nontechnical support staff. I know from the research I've done that yours is an innovative, cutting-edge young firm. My skills and abilities are a good match with your growing needs. I look forward to being part of your team and growing with you."

In his short introduction, this applicant managed to tell the interviewer a great deal about himself, his abilities, his personality, and his desire to work for this company. Your introduction needs to have these same elements in it.

QUESTION: "WHAT WAS THE WORST JOB (OR BOSS) YOU EVER HAD?"

Don't say anything bad about a past employer. It will only make you sound like you're not a team player. Everyone knows there are unpleasant jobs and terrible bosses in the world. A professional gets the job done no matter what.

Sample Answer

"I've enjoyed every job (or boss) I've had. Although they were very different, I learned specific things from each that helped me develop my professional skills. As I became more experienced, I enjoyed the jobs that gave me more responsibility and challenged my problem-solving abilities. In my last job, I solved a problem we had in filling customer orders in a timely fashion. *(Here you explain how you solved this problem)*. I applied for this position because it's time for new challenges and I know this company is constantly expanding."

Question: "Where Do You See Yourself in Five Years?"

Don't tell your interviewer that you plan on being an astronaut unless you really don't want the position he's got open. Stay focused on meeting the company's needs and staying rooted within it for the foreseeable future. Your long-term objective should include the opportunity to work in an arena where you can grow professionally and accept bigger responsibilities and challenges.

Sample Answer

"Right now I'm interested in the position you have in your receiving department. I have the skills and experience for it. I spent five years working part time during college in the receiving department of a local Coscos. I know from my research that this is a diversified company, so I believe that there will be many opportunities for my professional growth within your organization."

Question: "What's Your Greatest Shortcoming?"

No one, absolutely no one, is perfect. Your objective here is to take a negative and present it in a way that it becomes a positive. The following answer demonstrates one candidate's ability to take criticism and benefit from it.

Sample Answer

"In my last job I had problems the first few days on the job balancing out my cash register drawer at the end of the day. My supervisor took the time to review the process with me and show me the mistake I was making. I really appreciated his help, and I learned not to be afraid to ask for help if I'm having a problem."

QUESTION: "WHAT ARE YOUR OUTSTANDING QUALITIES?"

This is a perfect opportunity to sell yourself. If you listened to the interview, you should know what he needs in the person who will fill this position. Tailor your response and match your skills with his needs. If the interviewer tells you during the interview that the position needs someone with organizational and computer skills, then play up your abilities in these areas using specific examples from your past experiences. Now is a perfect time to restate your strongest skills or characteristics.

INTERVIEW DO'S AND DON'TS

As you prepare answers to typical questions you might be asked, keep these points in mind:

- Listen carefully to every question the interviewer asks and take a moment to think before you answer.
- If you don't understand a question, ask for it to be repeated, rephrased, or explained.
- Don't try to avoid answering a question. A good interviewer always sees through a sidestep. Be direct and honest.
- Be prepared to defend your resume; the interviewer may want to discuss it in detail.
- Be prepared to explain gaps in your work history.
- Whenever you can, match your skills to the employer's needs.
- Show you solve problems, set goals, and accomplish them; give specific examples.
- Show how you saved a previous employer money and/or generated revenue for the company; give specific examples.
- Explain, with examples, how you are a team player.
- Say why you want to work for the company.

ILLEGAL QUESTIONS

Title VII is a Federal law that prohibits employers from discriminating against you on the basis of sex, race, religion, national origin, and age.

Most states forbid questions pertaining to physical or mental disability, marital status, arrest record, number of children you have, child care, and financial status. You can be asked these question only if there is a bona fide occupational qualification (BFOQ) within the requirements of the job.

If a job requires physical strength, then an employer may require a physical test as long as it is nondiscriminatory. If you've applied for a job that is specifically for a certain sex, such as a dressing room attendant, then your sex is a BFOQ.

Here are some illegal questions an interviewer *cannot* ask:
- Have you ever had a drug or alcohol problem?
- Which clubs, societies, or lodges do you belong to?
- Are you married, single, divorced, or separated?
- What was your maiden name (if a married woman)?

Here are some legal questions an interviewer *can* ask:
- Where do you live?
- How long have you lived in this state or city?
- Are you a citizen of the United States?
- Do you have the legal right to work in the U.S.?
- Do you possess a valid driver's license? (He can ask this question but it's illegal to require that you produce a driver's license.)
- How many languages do you speak or write fluently? (He can ask this question, but it's illegal to ask, "What is your native language?" or to ask how you acquired the ability to read or speak a foreign language.)
- Have you been convicted of a crime? (He can ask this question, but it's illegal to ask if you've ever been arrested.)

WHAT TO DO WHEN AN ILLEGAL QUESTION IS ASKED

Although you can refuse to answer an illegal question, it's rarely in your best interest. When one comes your way, take a minute to think about your response and don't react negatively or back away from the question. Try to turn the question around to your advantage. Most of the time it's better to answer the question without telling the employer more than he needs to know. Here's how one applicant handled an illegal question:

An interviewer noticed an engagement ring on the finger of 22-year-old Maria Rodriguez. He asked, "I see you're getting married. Do you intend to have children?" Although the question is not legal, the interviewer was concerned that all the money spent hiring and training her would be wasted if she decided to get pregnant and leave the company.

Maria responded, "Although I plan on having children someday, those are future plans. I've invested a great deal of time and money in my education and in developing the skills necessary for this position. I'm excited about starting my career here. I intend to give it my all."

Maria turned the question around to her advantage—to stress her commitment to her career—and that's what you must do. After the interview, you can determine the motive for asking the illegal question. If the question still makes you feel uncomfortable, then this is not the company for you.

YOUR TURN TO ASK THE QUESTIONS

If, during the interview, you have a question, then ask it. Sometimes you need to ask one so you can answer an interviewer's question more appropriately. Remember, an interview is a two-way conversation. You and the interviewer are getting to know each other.

Don't come into an interview without a list of questions to ask, and don't leave without asking them, especially questions specifically about the company, ones that demonstrate your research and knowledge of the company. This shows how interested and enthusiastic you are about the job.

At the end of the interview you may be asked, "Do you have any questions?" Never say, "No, you were very thorough in your description of the job." You sound disinterested to the interviewer. Show your interest and concern in the job by asking some relevant questions, even if you're not asked if you have any.

Here are some questions you might want to ask:
- What is the most important part of this job?
- Is there a problem that needs immediate attention?
- Is this a new position or am I replacing someone?

- Could you describe my responsibilities?
- Who will I be reporting to?
- Is there any in-house training that is available?
- What skills do you think are important for this position?
- Are performance reviews given, and how often?
- How long do you estimate it takes for an individual to become proficient in this position?
- Do you promote from within when a position becomes available?
- What characteristics do your best employees have in common?

Here are some questions you should never ask:
- What type of medical benefits are available?
- How much vacation and sick leave will I be entitled to?
- How soon can I expect a raise?

Questions pertaining to salary or benefits are never discussed at an interview unless the interviewer introduces them. You may ask these questions after the job is offered to you, and before you accept.

IN SHORT

This chapter showed you many of the possible questions you might be asked and gave examples of answers, which can help you prepare yours. In the next chapter you will put it all to use when you rehearse in a mock interview, and again when the real interview takes place.

CHAPTER | 16

It's interview time: Get ready, get set, market yourself! This chapter will help you prepare to give that winning performance by telling you what to do in an interview and how to practice by having a mock interview.

INTERVIEW TIME
GIVING A WINNING PERFORMANCE

An interviewer knows within the first five minutes if a candidate is a winner. A great candidate sets a positive tone from the moment the interview begins. Both interviewer and applicant enjoy the conversation as they get to know each other. Stories, even jokes, are told. It's hard for you to believe that people have fun and laugh during an interview, but they do.

The mood is energizing. Everything is positive and all problems are solvable. Time flies and a 30-minute interview turns into an hour one. A great candidate has a dynamic personality and leaves an impression that lasts after the interview is over.

You're going to be part of a workplace family, so they need to like you. Sure, you were invited to come in for an interview because of all the skills and expertise you listed on your resume. But an interviewer doesn't hire a skill; she hires a person. When an interviewer likes you, she believes that you can overcome any weaknesses you may have. Let that wonderful personality you have shine during your interview so you'll be remembered, no matter how many others also interviewed for the job.

GOOD IMPRESSIONS COUNT

While you're waiting for the interview to take place, be pleasant to the receptionist or secretary who greets you. She is an important contact. Having someone remember you as the nice person with a smile and personality to match can't possibly hurt and can certainly help. Lots of smaller organizations pay attention to input from support staff. Consider her your first interviewer, so to speak. Besides, she is one more person to add to your network.

INTO THE LION'S DEN

The door to the interviewing room opens, your name is called, and you are invited in. Smile and offer your hand for a firm but not a crippling handshake. (Practice shaking hands with both a male and female friend.) You want a confident handshake, not a bone-crushing one. You definitely do not want a "limp lettuce" handshake.

Repeat the person's name out loud as you enter the interviewing room, and call the person by name during the interview. If there are several individuals interviewing, they will be introduced to you, one by one. Unless you've got a great memory, you won't remember all the names. Do acknowledge each introduction, look directly at the person, and repeat his or her name. Write down the names of your interviewers before you leave the room. If you forget, then ask the receptionist or secretary. You need these names so you can write thank-you notes after the interview.

BODY LANGUAGE

When the introductions are over there will usually be some small talk about the weather or the commute before the actual interview questions begin. This is a good time for you to take stock of your body language.

Sit comfortably in the chair, the small of your back pressed into it so that you sit up straight and tall, no slouching. Place both feet on the floor, feet crossed if that makes you more comfortable. Don't cross your legs unless your skirt or socks are long enough. Place your hands in your lap if you have a tendency to "talk" with them. Lean slightly forward toward the interviewer. Don't fold or cross your arms. Don't nod your head endlessly in agreement.

Body language is very telling. Send the right message—one that says you are alert, ready to participate in this conversation, and interested in everything.

Make eye contact. Look the interviewer asking the question straight in the eye when you answer. If there are other interviewers in the room, take a moment to look directly at each one of them as you're answering a question, but always return to the person who asked it.

GET OFF TO A GOOD START

Prepare a short summary about yourself for that frequently asked opening question, "Tell me about yourself." You need to be concise and direct. An employer usually knows within the first five minutes of an interview whether or not she is interested in you as an employee. Summarize the talents and values you have that make you the ideal candidate. Here's how one candidate described himself and made a good first impression:

"I'm an energetic, organized, problem-solver. My employers (or professors) have always considered my interpersonal skills and attention to detail to be two of my greatest assets. My enthusiasm for my work is contagious, and I have always been a good team leader. I believe in getting a job done in a timely manner but without sacrificing quality. My skills and work ethic make me a perfect candidate for this position."

You could follow this up with a question of your own: "What qualities are *you* looking for in an employee?" Listen carefully to the answer so you can tailor your answers during the rest of the interview to meet the employer's needs and expectations.

INTERVIEWING TIPS

The most important rule of all is *Smile.* You want to project an upbeat attitude. Then sit tall and walk tall. Make the first impression the interviewer gets of you a positive one. Remember the following:

- Don't accept coffee, tea, soda, or even water if it is offered; having a drink is a distraction you don't really need right now.
- Show enthusiasm for your work (even if you're not *that* excited about it).
- Listen carefully to the questions asked. Pause for a moment before answering.
- If you don't understand a question, ask for it to be repeated or rephrased.
- Think of this interview as a two-way conversation where you and the interviewer are getting to know each other.
- Make sure that by the end of the interview you've gotten across your strongest skills or characteristics. Be specific.
- Ask intelligent questions of your own. If you've done your research about the company, then this should be easy. These questions are important; they show you're really interested in working there. You want to leave a positive, enthusiastic image of yourself in that interviewing room. There's lots of competition, so give them a reason to hire you.
- Leave the interview with a good closing impression—a firm handshake, good eye contact, a "Thank you," and closing remarks like, "I'm very interested in this position," or "When can I expect to hear from you?"

DEALING WITH A DIFFICULT INTERVIEW

If you are interviewed by someone who is inexperienced or inept, just relax and don't get nervous. If the interviewer talks nonstop, wait for a break and then ask about the requirements of the job. Then stress how your qualifications fit the position. If there are long silences while the interviewer thinks about the next question, *don't talk.* Just wait until the next question is asked. Silences can be awkward, but if the interviewer is using the time to think, then he's not as aware of the conversation gap as you are.

An interview is a conversation between employer and applicant. You both have the opportunity to look each other over. An employer may want to hire you, but you may not want the job, and you do, after all, have the option of turning it down. Work is an important part of your life. Don't take a position if you don't want to do the work involved. Don't accept a position if you decide that the company culture is just not right for you.

Remember, every interview you survive, good or bad, is a learning experience that helps you improve your performance and be ready for that perfect job.

TRUE STORY

Don't Try to Impress with Titles

Linda responded to an advertisement for a position as director of a halfway house for young homeless women. She had five years' experience in the field, as well as the professional certifications required for the position.

During her interview, she discussed each of her previous jobs in great detail. She spoke in a monotone voice, and neither her tone nor attitude conveyed any enthusiasm for her present job. She also spent a great deal of time talking about her job title and how she was ready to assume more responsibility and have a *better* job title. She seemed obsessed with convincing her interviewers that she was ready for this upward move. She constantly reminded them that her duties included responsibilities not listed in her "job title." She used the term "job title" over and over again. Her interviewers were left with the impression that her only concern was a title with more prestige than the one she had.

Don't be like Linda. Forget about titles and concentrate on selling your interviewer on your enthusiasm and ability to get the job done.

THE MOCK INTERVIEW

Now that you have reviewed the interviewing basics, it's time to put yourself to the test. A mock interview is a safe way to try everything you've learned and a great way to iron out the kinks in your presentation. Here's how to do it:

- Get a friend to be your interviewer and another to be an observer.
- Give your "interviewer" a copy of your resume and the job description you've applied for.
- Give her the list of questions suggested in Chapter 15, but encourage her to add some of her own questions as well.
- Dress for the interview. This is a perfect time to try out that new outfit and make sure you're comfortable in it.
- If you can, videotape or, second best, audiotape the practice session.

TRUE STORY

Making the Most of an Awkward Interview

A young woman applied for a secretarial position in a large nursing home. After the personnel office reviewed her application and she passed the necessary preliminary steps, she was sent to the head of the housekeeping department, the man who would be her supervisor if she were hired. The interviewer wore sunglasses during the entire interview. He stood the whole time and didn't invite the applicant to sit down. He didn't ask any questions about the woman's previous work experience but instead talked at great length about himself.

If you were the applicant, would you ask him to remove his glasses and ask if you can sit down, consider yourself lucky not to have any tough questions to answer, or perhaps try to save the interview by asking questions yourself?

The young woman asked questions about the position, but, as she left, she asked *herself* a question: "Do I really want to work for this person?"

After the interview is over, have the observer and interviewer fill out the observation form on the next page. Then discuss their reactions to your responses. Finally, evaluate yourself. Do this before you view or listen to the tape. Afterwards make notes on what you want to change. Then do it all over again. Practice makes perfect.

IN SHORT

In the last three chapters you learned a great deal about preparing for and surviving the interview. The next chapter focuses on what to do *after* the interview is over. You'll write a thank-you letter and analyze your interview performance so you can continue to refine your interviewing technique.

Mock Interview Checklist

Did the job applicant: Have a firm handshake _____
Make good eye contact _____ Smile _____
Dress appropriately _____ Have a good attitude _____

How would you rate the applicant's overall appearance? _____

_____

_____

By the end of the interview, did you know what the applicant's skills and abilities were? _____

_____

How did the applicant answer questions about his or her technical skills? _____

_____

How did the applicant answer questions about his or her schooling
and career? _____

_____

Did the applicant show enthusiasm for the job? How? _____

_____

What did the applicant say that impressed you? _____

_____

What did the applicant say that didn't make a good impression?

_____

Would you hire this applicant? Why or why not? _____

_____

_____

_____

CHAPTER | 17

What comes after the interview? A follow-up letter and maybe a call, an assessment of your interview performance, and, if you don't get an offer, steps to take that will turn a disappointment into more opportunities.

IT'S NOT OVER YET!
AFTER THE INTERVIEW

You've had the interview, and you think it went pretty well. You can sit back and relax now, right? Wrong! There's still lots of work for you to do. Follow-up activities are just as important as the steps that have led you this far in your job search.

THANK-YOU LETTERS

Don't wait. Write a thank-you no later than the day after your interview. Send one to each person who interviewed you. A good thank-you letter shows your interest in the job to whomever is in the position to hire you.

Perhaps you walked out of the interview and said to yourself, "I wish I had mentioned . . ." or "I forgot to talk about. . . ." Thank-you letters provide a second chance to speak to your interviewer. They let you remind him one more time how valuable an employee you'll be or give you the opportunity to clarify a point you didn't quite make.

Sometimes you leave an interview knowing that you're not getting the job, as your skills just don't match the needs of the employer. You should still write a thank-you letter. Don't hesitate to ask for future consideration in a position that may be more appropriate. You could even ask for a referral to another company where your skills would be a better fit.

WHAT TO PUT IN THE LETTER

Begin your letter by thanking the interviewer for his time. Express your pleasure in meeting him and your enthusiasm for the position. This is your opportunity to reemphasize how your skills and experience make you the perfect candidate for this position.

If you need to clarify something that was said or misunderstood during the interview, this is the place to do it. Also include any additional information your interviewer requested. Ask questions you may still have. In general, if there's anything you forgot to tell your interviewer that puts you in a favorable light for the position, then include it here.

There's no need to write a long letter; keep it short, like the one in the sample at the end of this chapter. One page is sufficient. Be enthusiastic in your tone and use strong, positive action words to say once more how much you'd like to work for the company and what you have to offer in terms of skills and knowledge. To remind him of your interview, include a reference to something that was said in your conversation.

To make a good impression remember to:
- Spell all the names and titles correctly.
- Check your overall spelling and grammar and have a friend check it for you.
- Use standard business format when typing it. Don't hand-write this letter.

ANALYZE YOUR PERFORMANCE

Every interview you have is important because it allows you to practice all that you've learned. Each interview is a tune-up in your long-term interviewing performance. After the interview, take a few minutes to jot down your own reactions to the interview, using the checklist below. Be honest in your self-appraisal. Look for any negative factors. Often you know exactly the moment you've shot yourself in the foot. Determine what went wrong and then fix it before your next interview.

Think about what you said and what the interviewer said during the interview. What hypothetical problems did the interviewer bring up and how did you solve them? Did the interviewer have objections about hiring you, and did you try to overcome them? For instance, did he suggest you might be too young or inexperienced? Did you have good, reassuring responses?

Interviewing well is a skill you can learn and perfect. The day will come when your interview will get you the job you really want.

POST-INTERVIEW CHECKLIST

Take a few minutes to think back to your interview and make a critical analysis of it, using these questions as your guide:

Was my overall appearance and attitude positive? _____

Did I establish a rapport with my interviewer? _____

What was the general tone of the interview? _____

_____

Did I really express my enthusiasm for the position? _____

_____

Did I adequately discuss my skills and abilities? _____

_____

How did I answer questions? _____

_____

Did I address the interviewer's concerns? Did I meet his needs?

_____

_____

Which questions did I have trouble answering? _____

_____

_____

What areas need to be improved? _____

_____

WHEN YOU DON'T GET A RESPONSE

If you don't hear from the employer, give her a call. Check if the interviewing process is still going on. Be friendly and upbeat. She may have narrowed the field and you're still in the running. Ask if there's any information you can provide that would help her decide. Find out what stumbling blocks might be in your way, and resolve them if possible.

If she's chosen another candidate, try to get feedback about your interview so you can adjust your pitch for the next round.

WHY APPLICANTS ARE REJECTED

There are many reasons an interview doesn't result in a job offer. The interviewer may think that the applicant:

- Lacked the skills to perform the job
- Was unable to answer questions clearly and concisely
- Didn't project a successful profile and lacked poise or confidence
- Was overly aggressive; personality wouldn't fit with team
- Was unprepared and asked few if any meaningful questions; lack of research about the company
- Was unable to explain unfavorable factors in a resume, such as employment gaps or lack of degree
- Had unrealistic expectations about the salary; was more interested in salary/benefits than the job

Almost all these interviewing problems could have been avoided by taking the time to prepare and practice before the interview. The mock interview in Chapter 16 is a particularly useful way to evaluate the overall image you project.

Remember, it's not necessarily the candidate who is the most qualified who gets the job. It's the applicant who convinces the employer that she can do the job and become a dynamic part of the company team. The formula to success is part skills and part personality, so let yourself shine.

Oops, You've Been Rejected

Actors and job applicants have much in common. Both are always trying to sell their special talents and both are subject to lots of rejections. Sometimes an employer won't tell you why you weren't chosen, but it's a smart idea to call and ask why. Perhaps there's something you did that you can change for the next interview. Often it's just because there were several qualified candidates and the interviewer simply had to choose one and reject the rest.

Keep interviewing. Make rejection a learning experience. It's in your court to figure out what went wrong. Go back to the mock interview checklist you'll find at the end of Chapter 16. This time review your performance from the interviewer's viewpoint.

Keep Knocking on the Door

If you've been turned down for a position in a company that you really want to work for, then stay in touch and work your contact person. Periodically call or write a short upbeat note. Be persistent, but not a pest. Persistence often pays off, especially if the people you met liked you. If the objections to hiring you were issues you were able to correct, then drop the interviewer a note, reminding her about your strengths and what you've done to build up your weaknesses. It's up to you to overcome your employment disabilities.

Once you start job hunting, stay focused on the process. It's easier to deal with rejection if you've got other interviews scheduled. The right job is waiting for you somewhere. Polish your pitch, and keep working toward your goal.

Everything Was Wonderful—But I Didn't Get the Job!

When you've interviewed well, you know it. It's like singing a song and hitting all the right notes. But sometimes even a great performance doesn't get you the job. Often there are other forces at work.

For instance, perhaps the company had an employee interviewing for the position who had an insider's advantage over you. There's nothing you can do to get this job. Just consider it an exercise in learning how to interview well.

Or maybe the company really liked you, but you're lacking one key component for the position—a skill or asset that another candidate has. Use this to your advantage. If you really want to work for this company, then stay in touch. If they like you, there's a strong possibility you'll be hired for another position that requires your skills.

TRUE STORY

Opportunity Can Knock More Than Once

Sheila interviewed for a position as a director of a large group home for homeless women. She had lots of experience working in the shelter system. She also had all the educational requirements needed for the position. She was poised and confident during her interview, despite the fact that there were five people asking questions.

Sheila worked a full-time as well as a part-time job. Her part-time position involved caring for late-stage AIDS patients. She really impressed the interview committee with her work ethic, enthusiasm, empathy, and sincerity. But, unfortunately, she did not have any managerial experience. The new position involved overseeing ten staff members, and there were many problems in the office that required the skills and wisdom of an experienced manager.

Although Sheila was not hired for the position, the committee kept her resume on file because they liked her. Several months later, a resident manager position became available. The job was perfect for Sheila. It was an appropriate next step for her to develop her management skills. The committee was delighted to offer her the position.

In Short

Sometimes a response like, "Even though we can't offer you the position, we'll keep your resume on file" really *does* mean the doors are kept open—perhaps to a job that's ultimately better suited to your assets and interests. Keep your options open by following up, even after an interview that doesn't land you a job. A thank-you letter is the first and most important piece of follow-up you can do.

But don't sit around playing the waiting game. Keep all your present options open, and work to generate new ones. After all, you're in it for the long haul, as the next chapter makes clear.

A Sample Thank-You Letter

June 20, 1997

Joseph Mazulli
Vice President
Computer Designs
62-13 Foxhollow Road
Springfield, New Jersey 08008

Dear Mr. Mazulli:

It was a pleasure to meet you and the members of your development staff, Ms. Ruth Glenn and Mr. Robert Saunders, on Friday, January 31. Thank you for the opportunity to visit your new offices and to observe first-hand the exciting new technological advances your company is making in the area of voice-activated computers for the visually impaired.

I'm excited at the prospect of being able to use my experience in software design to help develop new products with your company. My customized software helped Dr. Friedman create the multimedia lab for physically handicapped students at Riverdale College. It was a challenging experience. Most of the improvements we invented are only just appearing in the marketplace. I've enclosed a copy of my final written analysis of the project as you requested.

I look forward to continuing our dialogue about emerging technological changes and being part of your team to make them happen.

Sincerely,

Ramon Luiz

As you have already discovered, not every interview leads to a job offer. On the contrary, looking for a job is hard work, and getting rejected for a job is hard on the ego. There are ways to avoid the squashed raisin syndrome, as you'll discover in this chapter, with its practical tips to help you maintain your positive attitude for the long haul.

THE LONG HAUL
MAINTAINING YOUR POSITIVE ATTITUDE

J ob hunting takes time. Finding the right job, one that you can start building a career from, doesn't happen overnight.

Rejection is also part of the process. It's both normal and expected. If there are 30 candidates for the job and only one opening, then you can do the math yourself: 29 candidates will be rejected. Many of those 29 people are qualified for the job, so you're in good company. Don't look at it as just a rejection; think of it also as a learning process. Every interview allows you to develop the skills necessary to land the *right* job in your future.

BELIEVE IN YOURSELF

There are lots of people looking for employment. Some of them may have more experience or be better educated than you. That doesn't matter. The talents you bring to a job are unique, because after all, there's only one of you. Nothing attracts an employer more than a person with a good attitude. So believe in yourself and your abilities. Think and act like a winner and you'll be one.

BECOME A PROFESSIONAL ACTOR

Smile and smile again. Be cheerful. It doesn't matter that inside you don't feel confident or positive. No one knows but you, unless you're acting depressed and negative. Act more confident than you feel. If you can convince others, then you'll begin to believe it yourself. Take control of your life. Success is the ultimate confidence builder.

APPEARANCE COUNTS

Look neat and well groomed, even if you're just going to the corner store. One of the signs of depression is lack of interest in your personal appearance. You never know when or where you'll meet a networking contact.

MAINTAIN YOUR FOCUS

No matter what happens or how long it takes to find the right job, be determined. Olympic athletes win the gold by staying committed no matter what happens. It takes drive and determination to get the job you want. Set your daily goals and work toward them.

A STEP AT A TIME

Remember, each "no" you receive during the job-hunting process leads you one step closer to the "yes" you really want. Don't beat yourself up and ask, "Why haven't I found a job yet? What's wrong with me?" Nothing is wrong. Understand the process, and that it takes time, energy, and commitment. Don't succumb to depression; be mentally tough.

TIME MANAGEMENT FOR JOB HUNTING

Getting the right job *is* your job for the moment. Treat your day as if you were going to work. These are the minimal goals to accomplish each day and each week:

- Spend at least four days per week in serious pursuit of a job. Get up early and get started making your networking or follow-up calls.
- Make a master list of objectives for the day, including new networking calls as well as follow-up calls.
- Have lunch with a networking contact for an informational interview.
- Maintain your Job-Seeking Strategy Planning Record, found in Chapter 11. Keep track of every job, contact person, phone number, follow-up dates, and all the rest. It helps to maintain your record keeping on a daily basis. That way, information is at your fingertips when you need it.
- Set a goal of eight calls per day and reach out to five to ten companies each week.
- Don't let a week go by that you don't have two to three interviews scheduled. Even if the job you're interviewing for isn't your dream one, you can use the practice.
- Send your resume out again and again and again.

Don't procrastinate! Do everything listed above, *now*.

EXAMINE YOUR FINANCES

Review your monthly financial needs. Make a realistic budget and stick to it. Check your credit. Most creditors will work with you if you have problems meeting your financial obligations. School loans are the easiest to get deferred, but even credit card companies will work with you. It's important to keep a good credit rating even for a new graduate. Paying back school loans tells an employer about your integrity in meeting obligations, and banking firms often order a credit check on new hires who will be handling money.

DEALING WITH MONEY CONCERNS

When money is really a problem, then you must evaluate your options. Can you move back in with your parents until you get a job? Don't forget, it's their house, so be prepared to live by their rules.

Don't borrow money from your family or friends unless you're prepared to pay it back. Good relationships have been destroyed by someone reneging on a loan. You could draw up a contract with the lender agreeing to the repayment terms.

If your money situation is desperate, then take an emergency job to tide you over while you search. It's often easier to get a job when you already have one. You don't seem so desperate to the employer.

SUPPORT GROUPS ARE IMPORTANT NOW

You need emotional support you during your job hunt. A support group serves as your personal sounding board. More importantly, you need a cheerleader to help you get through the tough times, especially when you get rejected for a job, which you probably will. (Everybody does, at one time or another.) You can use the help in maintaining your mental health. It's good to vent your fears and frustrations in a supportive atmosphere so that you'll be upbeat for your interviews.

FORMAL GROUPS

Structured groups like the 5 O'Clock Club®, which was started by Kate Wendleton in New York City, exist across the country. The group in your area might have a different name. No matter; it will be a good source of moral support from other job seekers like yourself.

Essentially what these clubs do is provide a safe forum for job hunters to vent their fears and frustrations, to problem-solve, and to exchange job-hunting tips. Time spent together is very focused; there are no gripe sessions. Lots of useful information is shared. Everyone is both a coach and a cheerleader for each other. Check with local churches or state labor departments for a group that meets near you.

INFORMAL GROUPS

Support groups made up of your friends and family are also important. Just make sure the people supporting you understand that you really are looking for a job. Stay away from those individuals who constantly ask, "So when are you going to find a job?"

TAKE GOOD CARE OF YOURSELF

You've embarked on a stressful task, looking for a job. You've probably read or heard the following rules of life and ignored them. Now is the time to take them seriously. You want to be in fighting form so you can stand up against the competition. This is the job-hunting Olympics, so start training.

EXERCISE

If exercise was part of your normal routine, then continue. If it wasn't, then this is the perfect time to start. You don't need to join an expensive gym. You can do something that doesn't involve any special equipment or place, like walking, bicycling, or hiking. Start with 30 minutes a day. Exercise is a proven stress reliever and a good way to fight against depression because it releases endorphins, which are hormones that make you feel good.

DIET

Pay attention to what you eat. Not just because you want to look good, but because certain foods also maintain the serotonin levels in your brain, which help you fight depression. Go to the library and find a book about nutrition or ask your doctor. Eating well-balanced meals, not too high in fat or sugar, really does help you maintain your physical and mental health.

REST

Dark shadows won't improve your appearance for an interview. Get the rest you need. Keep the same hours you would if you were working. Fatigue hinders performance. You need to be at your best mentally as well as physically to get the job you want.

MAKE TIME FOR FUN

All work and no play is unhealthy. See a movie, take a walk, or hang out with your friends. It may be a cliché, but laughter really is good medicine. Stay away from depressing people. This is the time to stay motivated, so surround yourself with winners. A winner has a positive outlook and will reinforce your outlook on things. Attitude is everything!

KEEP BUSY

Don't waste time. When you're not looking, calling, or speaking to someone about a job, then do something useful. Volunteer for a charitable organization. First, it's a reminder that other people have even bigger problems than you. Second, volunteering can lead to a job. A position may open within the organization, or you might find one through the networking you'll do among all the new people you'll meet.

LEARN A NEW SKILL

It never hurts to be add something to your battery of talents. For instance, if you only know the Microsoft Office Suite software package, then this is a good time to start learning how to use another software package. Check the ads to see which programs employers require. It can't hurt to be proficient in Excel *and* Lotus 1-2-3.

Education is a lifelong commitment. Those who stay flexible and continue to develop new skills are the ones who will always be marketable.

WHAT TO DO IF IT TAKES TOO LONG

If you're seriously looking for an entry-level job, the general rule-of-thumb is that it should take you approximately one month for every $10,000 of salary. A $30,000 job should take no more than four months if you've targeted your campaign and are aggressively pursuing employment in an economically healthy geographic area. If your region has high unemployment statistics, then you can expect it to take more time. It's not impossible to get a job more quickly, though, since there are always jobs available, even in the toughest areas.

When the job hunt takes longer than expected, it's time to reevaluate. If you're not even getting an interview, then either your resume needs to be reevaluated or you've targeted the wrong field.

Stay Flexible but Committed

Jorge could't fing a job in his field after he wass laid off. Out of desperation Jorge did some research and discovered that there was a growing need for medical billers and coders. He took a certificate program at the community college nearby. His unemployment insurance ran out before the program was completed and he was forced to use his savings to survive. He became very depressed.

Jorge signed up fora free resume workshop at the community college. What did he have to lose? The workshop facilitator videotaped his mock interview and played it back for him. He was surprised to see all the negative messages he was sending. His posture was terrible, and his attitude was unpleasant. In general, he sent out a message that chased employers away.

He worked on improving his presentation. His facilitator suggested that he volunteer at a local hospital so he could develop new networking contacts.So he did.

One day he heard about a part-time opening in the hospital's medical records department, so he updated his resume to include his new skills and spoke to a hospital administrator who was one of his new networking contacts. A friend from the hospital helped him prepare for his interview. Two weeks later he was working as a medical biller/coder, and six months later he had a full-time job.

Jorge got himself on a promising new career track because he was committed to his career change and he accepted the advice of all the professionals who were willing to help him. He came out a winner.

REVIEW YOUR RESUME

Are your skills clearly listed? Does it use action words to describe you expertise? Is it focused on the specific industry in which you're searching for a job? Is it formatted in a reader-friendly way, or do you have to search to pick out your strengths? Have a friend review it also.

HAVE YOU PICKED THE RIGHT INDUSTRY?

If you're looking for a job in the computer industry and your resume doesn't list any expertise in the field, then you're hunting for a job without any credentials. Before you spend additional time looking for a job in that field, reassess your goals. You must be able to demonstrate some transferable skills to get a job in an industry in which you have limited experience. Perhaps you need to develop additional skills first.

RECONNECT WITH YOUR NETWORKING CONTACTS

Call all the people on your networking list. Tell them that your job search is stalled and ask for advice. Try to broaden the circle of contacts. Anyone you know, even if it's just a "good-morning" acquaintance, is part of your network. This is not the time to be shy.

CHECK YOUR INTERVIEWING SKILLS

If your resume gets you into the interview and you don't get called back for a second interview or offered a position, then reevaluate your interviewing skills. Review the chapters on interviewing, especially the section on the mock interview in Chapter 16. Practice will improve your skills.

IN SHORT

This is *your* life. Many of the suggestions in this chapter will help you, not just in your career, but throughout your personal life as well. Maintain your mental attitude. Stay determined. Project confidence—think and act like a winner. You know what you want and are determined to get it. Remember, *you* are you own knight in shining armor.

With persistence, you will eventually land the job you really want. And when you do, you'll find that the information in the next chapter will coach you in accepting a job offer and negotiating your salary.

CHAPTER | 19

You got the job. That's great! Before you accept the position, though, you owe it to yourself to evaluate the offer and negotiate for the best compensation package you can get.

CONGRATULATIONS!
NEGOTIATING THE BEST DEAL

I t's exciting to be offered a job, but don't jump into accepting the position until you've reviewed all the benefits in your financial package. Don't hang up the phone until you've thanked the interviewer and told him how excited you are about working for his company, *but* that you need a day to make the final decision. If you have other interviews still scheduled or have been offered another job, tell him. It may make you an even more desirable candidate and could lead to a better offer.

The truth is, you need the time to evaluate his offer before you accept, particularly if you've gotten another offer as well from another firm. Ask who in the company you can call to discuss the company benefits package. This is an important decision you're making, so give yourself the time to get all the facts first.

YES OR NO?

What if the person who's made you the offer insists on an immediate answer? If you really want the job, then say yes. If you don't, say thank you, but no. An immediate decision is difficult to make if you're not sure about working for the company, or if you still have interviews scheduled. Ask yourself the following questions:

- Are you uncomfortable working for a company that won't give you a day to ask more specific questions about company policy and benefits? If you absolutely don't want to work for them, then say no without hesitation.
- Do you need a job right now because you need the money? If your financial survival is the issue, then say yes. Even if the job turns out to be lousy, it's a good learning experience. It's also much easier to get a job while you have a job. Make sure you learn everything you can while you're there.
- Don't be frivolous in making your decision to accept or reject when an employer is pushing you to immediately accept his offer. And just because your initial response is yes, there's no law that says you can't change your mind.

HOW MUCH DID YOU SAY I'M MAKING?

Your salary isn't the only financial reward you receive from a job. You should evaluate the total compensation package to really assess the financial aspects of your new job. Then there are other related tangibles that you need to consider in order to arrive at a complete analysis of what you will be earning.

Read the following section and prepare questions before you call your new employer. You can only really know what you're accepting if you know exactly what you're being offered. In the end, your decision may be based on future growth potential instead of immediate monetary compensation. Remember to keep your tone and attitude friendly.

THE COMPENSATION PACKAGE

No matter what your age, you need to be realistic about your present and future needs. Every company offers a different package, from health insurance plans to vacation time. The following list will help you analyze how much you'll really be earning:

- How much is the salary? How often do you get paid?
- Are there any bonuses, commissions, or incentives? How and when do you earn them?
- Is there any profit-sharing? Stock options?
- Is there a pension plan?
- Is there medical coverage? What does it include? What is your contribution? What are the deductibles?
- Is life insurance and disability insurance available? Who pays for them?
- How much vacation, personal, and sick time do you get? How are they accrued?
- Is there tuition reimbursement?
- Are there any employee discounts?

OTHER ADVANTAGES

Often you don't realize that there are perks within a specific work environment that translate into a financial savings for you as a worker. This savings is just as real as the money in your weekly or biweekly paycheck.

- **Commuting.** If you're offered a position that's close to home, you need to estimate what the reduced travel time means to you in terms of money (as well as the gas and wear and tear on your car).
- **Clothing.** If you will be working in an informal atmosphere, you'll have reduced clothing costs.
- **Gym.** Today companies view gyms as part of a health and fitness program that ultimately reduces their health insurance costs. You don't need to be an executive to have privileges if the company has a gym on the premises.
- **Travel.** Salesmen often get travel expenses, and sometimes a company car comes with the territory. If the job requires travel, ask about reimbursements or the possibility of a company car.

- **Child Care.** Only the most progressive companies offer child care on the premises. If you're really lucky, you will have landed a job in one of these organizations.
- **Expense Account.** If you've been hired as a salesman or account representative, you may be entitled to an expense account. If you're given one, then you should find out what expenses are allowable.

TRUE STORY

Know What You're Worth

Your research about a job should always include the salary guidelines. They should be up to date and appropriate to your skills level. Otherwise, you'll either price yourself out of the marketplace or shortchange yourself. Take Jerry, for example.

Jerry had just graduated from college with a degree in computer science. He was an inexperienced programmer with lots of talent. His friend suggested that he talk to a recruiter who worked solely with the computer industry. She recognized his talent and helped him assemble a resume, then she arranged several interviews for him with her clients.

He was very enthusiastic about his work but was also inexperienced as a job hunter. The recruiter told him not to discuss his salary requirements but to let them make him an offer, and she coached him on how to handle the question.

When he interviewed and they asked him how much he expected to earn, he immediately answered with a salary that was $10,000 less than they had planned to offer him. They were delighted and hired him immediately.

NEGOTIATING THE BEST DEAL

A kid in a grocery store doesn't just stare at the candy, hoping it will jump into his hand; he asks for it. Unless you ask your new employer, you won't know if you can have a benefit that may be important to you. Decide what's important to you and talk to the decision-maker.

Let's say, for example, that your research shows that the average pay for the position is more than they're offering you. First try to negotiate your salary to match this average. If this is rejected, then ask if you can count on a review and a pay raise in six months if you've met your quotas or job goals.

Or, suppose the job requires a lot of traveling by car to take care of clients. You know that some salesmen have company cars. Ask how long you need to be with the company, or how much revenue you must generate before you'll be entitled to a business car. Negotiate for your travel expenses to be paid with the knowledge that the IRS allows a deduction on your income tax—31 cents per mile as this book goes to press—for business travel if you fit within its guidelines.

Negotiation is an art, just like interviewing. It also takes practice. As you move up the corporate ladder, your compensation package will improve and opportunities for negotiation will increase. Start developing these skills now.

MAKING THE FINAL DECISION

Evaluate all the items that might be in your financial package. Don't trivialize the financial meaningfulness of any one item. Just because it's not in your paycheck every week doesn't mean it might not have a substantial impact on your standard of living.

Whether you take the job or not will be based only partly on your assessment of the total financial package. You will also be influenced by your gut reaction, which tells you if this is the right place for you. If the job is a wonderful opportunity, a stepping stone to your future, then your decision must take that into consideration. Realistically look at both your present and future needs. Money alone is not a reason to accept a job offer.

Ask yourself:
- Is there growth potential for me within this company?
- Do I like the corporate culture?
- Will I be comfortable in this environment?
- Will the position be challenging and rewarding?

- Can I work with the team?
- Can I grow with the company? Do they promote from within?
- How are promotions or bonuses given?
- Am I taking the position only for the financial rewards?

TRUE STORY

The Power of Negotiation

Cindy was offered a job with a large local health care company, which initially offered her only $500 more than her present salary as an administrative assistant at a local college. She asked if they could reconsider their offer. Unfortunately, the pay scale and benefits for this position were fixed, but the company really liked Cindy and told her that they anticipated an opening in another division that had a better compensation package.

Four months later, she was offered the title of clerical supervisor, making $500 a year more than her initial salary and with the same benefits package she had at the college. She also negotiated a promotion after her three-month probation was over, to an executive assistant with a raise of $3,000. Cindy then negotiated for a salary review in six instead of twelve months. Instead, because of her good work, she got a promotion to facility manager and a $5,000 raise. Once again Cindy negotiated for a review in three months and a promise of a $2,500 raise if she met their expectations. In less than one year, she will have received a total $11,000 in raises.

Cindy is a super worker, so she deserves her success, but she might not have gotten it, or not have gotten it so quickly if she hadn't learned the power of negotiation.

ACCEPTING THE OFFER

If you've carefully considered the offer and have decided to accept, call the interviewer and enthusiastically accept the job. Agree on a starting date and briefly describe your understanding of the benefits package. You may want to ask for a letter confirmating of this agreement.

If You're Leaving a Current Job

If you're presently working, type a brief letter of resignation and hand-deliver it. Two weeks' notice is standard for most jobs. This relationship is part of your total network, and you never know when you might tap into it again, so end your current job on a positive note. If your old employer offers you a raise if you stay, reevaluate your reasons for leaving in the first place. It rarely helps your professional development to stay.

Or Are Being Considered by Another Firm

Notify companies still considering you for a position. Keep the lines of communication open with any firm that really interested you. Reiterate how impressed you were with the company but that you believe that you've made the right choice in accepting the new job offer at this time. Sometimes an offer from another company makes you a more desirable candidate and you just might receive a counteroffer if you were in the running for a position there. If this happens, re-read the section in this chapter, Evaluating the Compensation Package.

FINAL DETAILS

Finally, write thank-you letters to everyone in your network that helped you. Keeping up those contacts takes a little work on your part but you'll be using and adding to them for the rest of your life. Follow the same business format you used with cover letters and thank-you notes. Again, let someone proofread your correspondence before you mail those notes.

LAST HURDLE—DRUG TESTING

Remember the *Seinfeld* episode when Elaine applies for a position with a large company that required drug testing, and she tests positive? She persuades the employer to allow her to retest several times, only to fail it again and again. It isn't until the end of the episode that the mystery is solved: Elaine discovers that she's been eating poppy seed bagels every morning for breakfast and they've been triggering the positive test results.

It was very funny on TV—but it isn't in real life.

Drug testing has become an accepted practice by many corporations.

Approximately half of all Fortune 500 companies require some form of drug testing during the interviewing process or as part of the final selection process. Many civil-service jobs also require drug testing. Once hired, you are rarely subjected to a drug test again unless you show signs of abuse or work in field that requires checks.

False positives can occur because you may be taking legitimate medication or, like Elaine, inadvertently eating something that's quite innocent. Compounding this problem is the 5 percent inaccuracy rate that most drug-testing companies admit occurs.

PREVENTING A FALSE POSITIVE

Most companies will ask you to fill out a form indicating the legitimate drugs you may be taking at the time the test is administered. Don't leave out any over-the-counter drugs either. How long it takes for your body to process a drug depends on your body weight, so protect yourself and list any drug you've taken in the preceding three weeks. The implications for a false positive reading can be devastating for future employment.

IN SHORT

Now that you've carefully evaluated the reimbursement package and negotiated the best deal you could get for yourself, you're ready to start work. Your future lies ahead. There's advice in the next chapter that will lead you up that ladder of success and help you plan for your future.

CHAPTER | 20

Everything you do and learn on this job is preparation for the next one. Each job will take you up the ladder of the success, and your responsibility and earning potential will increase. Plan for the future the moment you start this job.

BUILDING A FUTURE
STARTING OUT RIGHT

During the first three months of your new job, your new boss will be getting to know you and taking note of your performance. In today's marketplace there is no hesitation to terminate a relationship with a worker who isn't living up to expectations. Since most companies have a ninety-day probationary period, this is a crucial time for you as a new employee.

GET TO KNOW THE WORK TEAM FIRST

During the first three months, keep a low profile and learn the office politics and pecking order. Find a secretary who can explain the chain of command. He or she will probably tell you lots more information that you can mentally store. Listen and learn but don't get involved in the politics.

Introduce yourself. Maintain a friendly and cooperative manner toward everyone. Be just as nice to the janitor as the CEO. Meet people but don't make friends, not yet. It takes time to really get to know someone before you become business friends and trust them.

LEARN THE CORPORATE CULTURE

There are lots of rules within a corporate environment, both formal and informal. Pay attention to them if you want to fit in and be accepted. Don't be embarrassed to ask questions. Ask "smart" questions, but don't pester your peers with too many of them or you'll appear incompetent.

Forms of Address

Does everyone call each other by first name? Do you use Mr./Ms./Mrs. when referring to supervisors? What is the accepted norm for this company? It's easy to offend a worker, particularly someone who is older than you or in a higher position on the corporate ladder. You're trying to make friends, not enemies. Pay attention to the little details and you'll earn respect.

The Unofficial Dress Code

If all the men in the office wear three-piece suits, then you'll stand out if you wear a sports jacket. You don't need to look like a clone and you do want to express your individual taste, but you don't want to look like an outsider. You're part of a new family; fit in without giving up your individuality.

The Chain of Command

Corporations are fairly rigid about adhering to their formalized structure. If you have a question but particularly if you have a complaint, follow the chain of command and speak to the appropriate supervisors. Eventually, you'll learn who the power players are, but for now pay attention to the organizational chart. Don't jump over your boss's head unless you want her to chop yours off.

Celebrations

The rules vary from company to company. It's not necessary to donate to every collection taken; you might not be able to afford them all. But don't ignore a coworker's birthday or any other special event that the office is buzzing about. A carefully chosen card or a single flower is an inexpensive way to say congratulations. Once again, this is your workplace family and you don't want to offend or slight anyone.

What Does the Boss Expect of You?

Make sure you're doing things the way your boss wants them done. Find out what her expectations are. Don't guess; ask what she considers important. If necessary, make a list of your job duties. Ask your supervisor for confirmation that you are on the right track. Remember, there is an expected learning curve, but on the same hand you must be demonstrating that you are achieving your goals.

BE PREPARED FOR WHATEVER LIES AHEAD

The future can look scary—or filled with adventure and challenge. The choice is yours. You can be ready for whatever it offers, so long as you live and work today by these guideposts:

- **Accept challenging assignments.** Keep reaching to expand your abilities. Accept assignments that will continue your professional development. Understand your role on the team and what you're responsible for producing.
- **Extend your network of professional contacts.** Start with your peers and work your way up. Collect business cards. Join a professional association and attend its functions. Then stay in touch with old and new contacts any way that feels comfortable, like a brief phone call just to say "hi," or a holiday card with a personal note. The best jobs are filled through networks, so be part of them.
- **Use your networking partners as a resource.** When you're having trouble getting information or solving a work problem, someone in your network may have the answer. At work you look smarter because *you* solved the problem.
- **Find a mentor.** Top executives often have a mentor—someone who is several levels higher on the corporate chart. Find someone whose judgment you trust.

- **Keep your resume up to date.** No, you're not necessarily looking for another job. Maintaining your resume means that you're keeping track of your new accomplishments. When promotion or review time rolls around, you'll be prepared to "brag" about them. And you'll be ready, just in case you hear about a position that's even more exciting than the one you have.

- **Keep up with technology.** You can have fantastic skills and abilities, but if you don't keep up with emerging technological advancements, you'll find the best positions out of your reach. Stay up-to-date with your computer software skills. Learn a language or a new software program. Start earning a college degree if you don't have one, or an advanced degree if you do. You don't need to be the best, but you need to stay in the mainstream.

- **Learn something new every year.** The competition is fierce. Marketplace survival dictates that you add new skills to your arsenal every year. Don't be complacent once you get a job; your job market survival depends on remaining competitive.

- **Keep an eye on your company's financial health.** It doesn't matter what department or position you're in, stay tuned into the big picture. A downsizing move may be good for the company but it's bad for the workers. There's an old adage, "Last one in, first one out." On the other side, if a company is expanding, then there's room for you to move into a better position. Your professional survival depends on your observations and interpretation of the health of your company.

BUILD FOR YOUR FUTURE

In the last 20 years, the employment market has changed dramatically. Long-term employment marriages rarely happen anymore, and job security no longer exists. Downsizing, up-sizing, right-sizing—they all mean the same thing, which is an employment marketplace that's in transition with needs that change rapidly.

Today's marketplace is like the American Wild West; it takes a rugged individual to survive. If you plan to survive and thrive in the twenty-first century, you've got to be prepared to travel tried-and-true roadways as well as forge through scary new terrain. Complacency is an obscene word in this marketplace. Stay alert to emerging technologies and market trends and the future is yours!

CONCLUSION

Armed with self-knowledge, a great-looking resume and cover letters, job hunting savvy, and polished interviewing techniques, you're ready to face the world. And the world is waiting for you with open arms.

Only there's a baseball bat in each hand.

We never told you it would be easy. We never said it would be fun. But there is nothing like the feeling of self-confidence and accomplishment that come with hard work. If you've done the work, completed the exercises, and embraced the knowledge, you should be ready for whatever lies ahead. There should be no challenge too great, no job too removed from your grasp if you want it badly enough.

What you've learned here in this book you will use throughout the rest of your life. The job you'll be getting soon will not be your last. Like millions of others, you'll be involved in the job search process again, maybe several times more. It's true for us all; indeed, it's a fact of life these days. You've got to have the ability to successfully change jobs and even careers. It's part of working. You've got to be flexible, knowledgeable, and marketable. You have to take your package of skills and abilities and redefine it, whenever you're called upon to do so.

Success is that sweet meeting of personal and professional fulfillment, where your needs, values, and interests all intersect. It is the final crest of the hill, where you look down and say, "I did it. I made it. I'm finally there."

This book can't change your life. No book really can. Rather, it was designed to help you draw the map that shows "you are here"—and "there" is where you want to be. It gave you the directions and landmarks to guide you, and red flags to warn you of roadblocks and dead ends.

We wish you a good journey and a bright future!

There are many books, directories, periodicals, and even computer software and World Wide Web sites mentioned throughout this book that will be useful to you in your job search. We've put together here in one list those that we find particularly helpful.

ADDITIONAL RESOURCES

CAREER EXPLORATION

Bolles, Richard Nelson. *What Color is Your Parachute?* Ten Speed Press, 1997. The classic in its field: a practical manual for job hunters and career changers of all levels.

Research & Education Association, *Careers for the '90s.* 1994. Over 250 careers are described in detail, offering information on earnings, job descriptions, required education and training, advancement opportunities, and future job outlook.

U.S. Department of Labor, *Dictionary of Occupational Titles.* U.S. Government Printing Office, 1993. The DOT is the most comprehensive classification system available. It provides detailed information for over 20,000 occupations.

U.S. Department of Labor, *Occupational Outlook Handbook*. U.S. Government Printing Office, 1996. An easy-to-use handbook that can be used in conjunction with the DOT. Occupations are broken down by topics, such as nature of the work, job outlook, salary, qualifications, etc.

EDUCATION AND TRAINING FOR CAREERS

Farr, J. Michael. *America's Top Jobs for People Without Degrees*. 3rd Edition. JIST Works, Inc., 1996. Up-to-date descriptions for 111 major jobs, detailing earnings, growth projections, training required, and working conditions.

Rowe, Fred A. *Career Connection for College Education*. JIST Works, Inc., 1994. A guide to 100 college majors and their career opportunities.

INDUSTRY INFORMATION

Gale Research, *Encyclopedia of Associations*. Published annually, this multi-volume set lists 25,000 organizations and associations, with information about membership, publications, purpose, meetings, contact address, and phone number.

Magazines, such as *Times, Forbes, Business Week,* and *Crain's*. Published on a weekly basis, these magazines can be bought at newspaper and magazine stands and through subscription.

Newspapers, such as *The Wall Street Journal, Los Angeles Times, Boston Herald, Washington Post,* and *New York Times* publish daily business sections, and many other newspapers publish weekly business sections, usually on Sundays.

The Office of Management and Budget, *Standard Industrial Classification,* 1987. The SIC is a compilation of all industries, divided into ten major categories, for easy referencing. This government publication helps you choose an industry by showing the relationship of careers within industry groupings.

RESUMES

Beatty, Richard H. *The Resume Kit.* 3rd Edition. John Wiley, 1995. A comprehensive guide to resume writing for all levels of job seekers.

Rosenberg, Arthur D. and David Hizer. *The Resume Handbook.* Adams Media Corp., 1996. Descriptions and samples of resumes and cover letters for all types and levels of job seekers.

Yate, Martin John. *Resumes that Knock 'em Dead.* 2nd Edition. Adams Media Corp., 1995. Easy-to-follow directions on resume and cover letter writing, with many samples.

JOB HUNTING

Ferris, Donna MacDougal. *The Practical Job-Search Guide.* Ten Speed Press, 1996. A step-by-step guide, with chapters on budgeting, coping with changes in your relationships, and other practical advice.

Wendleton, Kate. *Through The Brick Wall: How to Job-Hunt in a Tight Market.* Villard Books, 1992. Written by the founder of the Five O'Clock Club, a job-search strategy group, this book is particularly useful for the long-term unemployed worker.

Adams, Bob. *The Complete Resume & Job Search Book for College Students.* Adams Media Corp., 1992. A comprehensive job-search guidebook for recent and soon-to-be graduates.

The 1997 Metropolitan New York Job Bank. Adams Media Corp., 1997. Job Bank is a detailed listing of employers indexed by industry. The Metropolitan New York Job Bank covers New York, New Jersey, and Connecticut. Companion publications offer information on 29 other geographic areas of the U.S.

THE INTERNET: WEB SITES

The AT&T College Network, *http://www.att.com/college*
AT&T's new web site, which posts job openings and career advice.

The Monster Board, *http://www.monster.com*
The Monster Board offers more than 52,000 job postings from top national companies such as Intel, Nike, United Airlines, MCI, etc. Jobs range from chief financial officer to entry-level positions.

Adams Job Bank Online, *http://www.adamsjobbank.com/*
America's Job Bank, *http://www.ajb.dni.us/*
America Net Worldwide Classified Ads,
    http://www.americanet.com/World-Ads/
Career City, *http://www.career-city.com/*
Career Mosaic, *http://www.careermosaic.com/*
Career Path.com, *http://www.careerpath.com*
Career Shop, *http://www.tenkey.com/careershop.htm*
Career Web, *http://cweb.com/homepage.html*

All these web sites have good things to offer job seekers, from career decision-making, positions available, resume writing, and interviewing tips, to networking.

INDEX

Order Form

CALIFORNIA

___ @ $35.00   CA Police Officer
___ @ $35.00   CA State Police
___ @ $35.00   CA Corrections Officer
___ @ $20.00   CA Law Enforcement Career Guide
___ @ $35.00   CA Firefighter
___ @ $30.00   CA Postal Worker
___ @ $35.00   CA Allied Health

NEW JERSEY

___ @ $35.00   NJ Police Officer
___ @ $35.00   NJ State Police
___ @ $35.00   NJ Corrections Officer
___ @ $20.00   NJ Law Enforcement Career Guide
___ @ $35.00   NJ Firefighter
___ @ $30.00   NJ Postal Worker
___ @ $35.00   NJ Allied Health

TEXAS

___ @ $35.00   TX Police Officer
___ @ $35.00   TX State Police
___ @ $35.00   TX Corrections Officer
___ @ $20.00   TX Law Enforcement Career Guide
___ @ $35.00   TX Firefighter
___ @ $30.00   TX Postal Worker
___ @ $32.50   TX Allied Health

NEW YORK

___ @ $30.00   NYC/Nassau County Police Officer
___ @ $30.00   Suffolk County Police Officer
___ @ $30.00   NY State Police
___ @ $30.00   NY Corrections Officer
___ @ $20.00   NY Law Enforcement Career Guide
___ @ $35.00   NY Firefighter
___ @ $30.00   NY Postal Worker
___ @ $35.00   NY Allied Health

ILLINOIS

___ @ $25.00   Chicago Police Officer
___ @ $30.00   Illinois Allied Health

FLORIDA

___ @ $35.00   FL Police Officer
___ @ $35.00   FL Corrections Officer
___ @ $20.00   FL Law Enforcement Career Guide
___ @ $30.00   FL Postal Worker
___ @ $32.50   FL Allied Health

MASSACHUSETTS

___ @ $30.00   MA Police Officer
___ @ $30.00   MA State Police Exam

The MIDWEST

(Illinois, Indiana, Michigan, Minnesota, Ohio, and Wisconsin)

___ @ $30.00   Midwest Police Officer Exam
___ @ $30.00   Midwest Firefighter Exam

The SOUTH

(Alabama, Arkansas, Georgia, Louisiana, Mississippi, North Carolina, South Carolina, and Virginia)

___ @ $25.00   The South Police Officer Exam
___ @ $25.00   The South Firefighter Exam

NATIONAL EDITIONS

___ @ $14.00   Civil Service Career Starter
___ @ $12.95   Bus Operator Exam National Edition
___ @ $12.95   Sanitation Worker Exam National Edition
___ @ $12.95   U.S. Postal Service 470 Battery Exam
___ @ $14.95   Armed Services Vocational Aptitude Battery

NATIONAL STANDARDS EXAMS

___ @ $20.00   Home Health Aide National Standards Exam
___ @ $20.00   Nurse's Assistant National Standards Exam
___ @$20.00   EMT-Basic National Standards Exam

To Order, Call TOLL-FREE: 1-888-551-JOBS, Dept. A040

Or, mail this order form with your check or money order* to:
LearningExpress, Dept. A040, 20 Academy Street, Norwalk, CT 06850

Please allow at least 2-4 weeks for delivery. Prices subject to change without notice

 ®L E A R N i N G E x p R E S S ®

An Affiliate Company of Random House, Inc.